# The Beauty of Stained Glass

## Patrick Reyntiens

A Bulfinch Press Book . Little, Brown and Company
Boston . Toronto . London

First North American Edition

First published in Great Britain in 1990 by
The Herbert Press, 46 Northchurch Road, London N1 4EJ

ISBN 0-8212-1811-5
Library of Congress Catalog Card Number 90-52566
Library of Congress Cataloging-in-Publication information is available.

Bulfinch Press is an imprint and trademark of Little, Brown and Company (Inc.)
Published simultaneously in Canada by Little, Brown & Company (Canada)
Limited

PRINTED IN HONG KONG

FRONTISPIECE
Autonomous panel, one of Three Sacred
Mountains; Calvary, by Patrick Reyntiens, 1974

# Contents

# Foreword

In writing this book I am conscious of being given the opportunity to review all that I hold to be beautiful in stained glass. Although 'beauty' is an almost superannuated word it still holds the clue to the puzzle. For it is the beauty of the medium, and of the creative minds behind it, that is the only justification for its coming into being. In writing a book about a subject that has been my primary concern and aim in life, I have been given the chance to refer to matters in history, architecture, the fine arts and aesthetics which have always fascinated me and given an added dimension to my own life. If this comes across in the book even minimally and in part, it will perhaps justify the writing of it.

When I started the book I had little idea how much I would be helped and encouraged by all my friends.

I should like to thank David and Brenda Herbert and their staff. To these should be added my editor, Curigwen Lewis and the designer, Pauline Harrison for their unfailing help. A book of this nature is nothing without its illustrations and for these, apart from the photographs I took myself, I owe above all an immense debt of gratitude to my friend Painton Cowen. I am much indebted to another friend, Andrew Moor, and also to Peter Cormack. The present-day artists whom I admire, among others far too numerous to mention, are Ray King, Ed Carpenter, Robert Kehlmann and Richard Posner. My English confrères are Rosalind Grimshaw, Douglas Hogg, David Wasley and Brian Clarke; to all of these I extend thanks for furnishing photographs to illustrate my thesis. Mrs Helene Weis of the Stained Glass Society of America kindly supplied photographs of Tiffany and LaFarge. The photographs (far too few, alas) of the great German artists Ludwig Schaffrath and Johannes Schreiter were taken by Ed Carpenter and Andrew Moor. I would especially like to thank Sandra and Michael Le Marchant for supplying and allowing me to include two photographs of my own work.

PATRICK REYNTIENS

# Introduction

Turner was heard to say 'Art's a rum thing' and this could quite easily be the motto of stained glass. It certainly has been the victim of a lot of misunderstandings, both as to how it can most effectively be used and how the medium came about in the first place. At the same time there is an aura of wonder hovering over stained glass, because it has such extraordinary associations throughout history. However, there *is* a tendency to dismiss it now as inappropriate for use in modern architecture. We are dealing with an art which has picked up a reputation today for being an irrelevant conundrum, too complex and involved technically ever to be fully explained or properly used.

There is so much misinformation about stained glass that I shall start this book by explaining, briefly, how it is made and how it evolved.

The commonest method of making stained glass is to carefully cut pieces of glass, fire them and then and set them in lead calms (sometimes called cames). The calms are small bars of lead so grooved on either side that the glass can be slotted in and held. Where the calms abut or join up they are neatly soldered together. The whole mass of interlocking lead and glass is gradually built up into a panel which, when it has been soldered on both sides, is a manageable unit. After making the panel watertight by means of a loose boiled-oil putty rubbed into the cracks and carefully cleaned off, it is ready to be assembled into a scheme of many panels, building up into a total window.

The craft of glass, indeed any craft at all, is a thing in itself. It is simply the best way of doing something, regardless of the actual

THE BEAUTY OF STAINED GLASS

point in history when this came about. Stained glass is not so much a medieval craft, as a craft that was brought to perfection in the Middle Ages. There is mention of its use as a medium in the fabric of Old St Peter's, Rome, built in the fourth century by Constantine. Whether the glass was the same age as the church is debatable, but it could have been. At Canterbury Cathedral the original twelfth-century leading was still – just – holding the glass together when the windows were releaded in the nineteenth century.

The custom of sedating light in great buildings, especially in the Mediterranean area, which has implacably fierce sunlight, is very ancient indeed. The great halls of the Pharaohs at Karnak and Luxor were glazed with thin alabaster slabs through which the light filtered, much stopped down by the honey-coloured opacity of the alabaster. Everything inside must have had a muted grandeur; all the bright greens, blues and reds of the Egyptian painted architecture were melded together by the unified golden light.

Nearer our own time, dating from around AD 430, the little tomb of Galla Placidia, in Ravenna, Italy, has such intense yellow alabaster slabs in the tiny windows that when the door is shut all the mosaics seem sub-aqueous green – yet when the door is open the mosaics stand out in a most glorious blue. Even as recently as the 1960s, the American firm of architects, Skidmore, Owings and Merrill, very successfully revetted the whole of the Beinicke Rare Book and Manuscript Library at Yale University with alabaster.

But Egypt was the cradle of glass making as of so many other arts and crafts. Whether Pliny's story of the invention of glass resulting from the kindling of a fire over naturally occurring soda sand is true, there is no means of telling; it seems likely enough now. However, the medium was quickly put to good use in the making of every conceivable vessel, bowl, bottle, jug and platter. By the end of the Roman Empire the glass industry was extensive and efficient.

Anything put into a window embrasure will modify the light coming through, even a sack or a rag. Oiled linen was used extensively before glass became commonplace in the Middle Ages. So was horn. In Byzantine times there certainly was some stained glass since it has been found in the course of archaeological digs in

Constantinople (Istanbul). It must have occurred to builders in Roman times that you could modify light coming into a building by means of coloured blinds or curtains draped across the window. What more logical step than that of making such a colour and tonal change permanent? The means was to hand, simply waiting to be used, in small sheets of glass.

Another reason for the use of stained glass, or its equivalent, over and above mere utility, was that, for certain purposes and in certain buildings, an atmosphere of reverence was necessary. As already mentioned the ancient Egyptians sedated the light coming into their major halls almost to the point of obscurity. Roman and Greek temples similarly were places of suspended disbelief, where the images of the gods were dimly apprehended. The connection between the sedation of light on the eye and the growth of the contemplative faculty in the mind seems always to have been known and acted on. The more bright light the brain receives the more instant the reaction – and the more the memorative faculty tends to recede. The less light there is in the interior of a building, the greater the extension of the memory.

The qualifying of light coming into a building is fairly straightforward. What calls for a leap of the imagination is the idea of putting the figurative element of a fresco or painting into the very source of light. This is where the art of stained glass begins to separate itself from the mere craft of keeping the weather out. As soon as any representation is incorporated as an element of design in glass it brings with it a range of associations and meanings that were inconceivable before. Apart from the question of the significance of the figuration (it could be an anecdote, a parable or a figure with depth of meaning such as a prophet or a saint) other qualities must be considered. The question of colour assumes an importance that it hitherto did not have in glass. What colour to use? What symbolic feeling was associated with it? Whether the mixtures of colours were inducive of this mood or that. All had to be decided and brought into play. Often the sheer unavailability of some colours was a factor bearing on decisions; much in composition by colour is inapplicable in stained glass because the strictly limited range of different shades and tones precludes the subtleties that are commonplace in painting.

The sensibilities of the early Middle Ages in Europe so far as colour was concerned were generally a carrying-through of those of the classical world, modified by the passing of time. What we do notice up to the middle of the twelfth century is a predominantly lyrical sense of colour. After the twelfth century, and for some hundred and fifty years, the lyricism turns to an altogether tougher and less sympathetic sense of colour.

Three factors came into the equation that made up the nature of stained glass. They were colour, drawing and interval. Colour can be efficiently divided between the lyrical and the constructional. In the lyrical approach to colour we are, as it were, invited into the imaginary world presented by art. The 'invitation' depends on the general harmony of all the colours used in the composition. Each colour draws for its character on each of the other contributing colours. Therefore since each colour has an affinity with its neighbours, there is an integral feeling of unity throughout.

Compare this with the alternative, which consists of separate areas of high-contrast colour being put together to exert the maximum vibrancy and clamour on the eye. This method of organization amounts to a call-to-arms. What is lost in subtlety and suggestion is compensated for by the energy and power released.

On an optical level what seems to happen is that in the first example the eye is happy to travel from the centre of one area of colour to the centre of an adjacent one. There is an invitation extended to the eye to browse around, as it were, and this 'invitation' principle is the basis for all lyricism in colour. In colour-as-drive-to-power the whole strength of the system lies in the meeting of the colours – and therefore the interaction on the frontiers of the colour is where the drama lies. The fierce vibrancy created makes an instant appeal, as opposed to the slower – and more long-lasting appeal of lyrical colour. The constant oscillation between these two methods of constructing colour from the twelfth century onwards contributes to making the history of stained glass so fascinating.

From the late classical times figuration was slow to develop. At the beginning stained glass design tended to follow the character of the major arts of the time. Up to the twelfth century these were manuscript illumination and personal jewelry, which was more often than not enamelled in brilliant colours. The sinuous designs in manuscripts were relatively easy to transfer to the design of stained glass. And the *cloisonné* or *champlevé* enamel techniques, with their neatly compartmentalized colour also lent themselves to being reproduced on a larger scale in stained glass. It was a case of the mental concepts that had hitherto been given expression in miniature things being reproduced on a larger format; a parallel development can be traced in many other large works of art.

Colour and drawing are straight forward. The question of interval needs more explanation. In glass the interval-structure, or how the colours are placed in relation to one another, between the stimuli of red or blue or white spread over the window, is what gives the whole composition its vitality. How the eye takes in one stimulus followed by another – and the time-interval between these stimuli – is in many ways parallel to how the ear perceives the intervals in music.

The fascination that number and proportion had for the twelfth century is another, less obvious, factor influencing the beginnings of stained glass. The adoption of the quadrivium as a pattern of higher education in the twelfth century underlines the enormous interest in making a harmony out of the phenomena of this world – and basing it all on mathematics. The quadrivium consisted in arithmetic, geometry, music and astronomy – not taught as separate but as inter-related subjects. It was believed that there was a basis for a mystical link between music, mathematical proportion and the heavens, according to popular philosophers of the time.

By way of bringing this introduction to an end I would mention two other aspects of the Middle Ages which were of crucial import-ance in the development of stained glass.

The use of the memory in medieval times was phenomenal. We can have an idea of the cultivation of memory by recalling the feats of some musicians in our time – Albert Schweitzer played the whole of the organ music of Bach at one sitting from memory. But in the Middle Ages, before the provision of artificial memory in forms of books, tapes, television and computers, there was only the human faculty to rely on. It was common for friars to be able to memorize the whole Bible; storytellers could (later) recite the whole of the *Divina Commedia*; the whole of Virgil's *Aeneid* could be quoted by some. The accumulation by the memory of a vast range of factors, sensibilities, instances, correlations, cross-references was taken for granted in those times. Memory was an essential tool for any kind of achievement. When applied to art this was of vital importance in providing continuity and stability. But it did not inhibit at the same time. Innovation and invention were not incompatible with an accurate and informed memory. They contributed to the second aspect I would like to mention – the habit of the medieval mind of making sideways leaps of reference and connotation. The mental habit of seeing analogies and similes between the animal and mineral and vegetable world and that of spiritual and moral values had considerable advantages. True, there were some pretty strange ideas circulating due to this form of cross-referenced associativeness, but the habit as a means of unifying all experience into a comprehensible whole did pay dividends, and not least in the sphere of art.

# The Twelfth and Thirteenth Centuries

## *The twelfth century*

An appropriate date from which to start an appreciation of the art of stained glass would be the coronation of Charlemagne on Christmas day AD 800 – a definitive juncture in our history. Charlemagne was crowned Emperor of the West in Rome by the Pope. The hope behind this move was the resuscitation of the Roman Empire in a new form. The new Emperor's capital in western Europe was Aachen, near the lower Rhine, but he looked towards Constantinople, the New Rome, rather than towards Old Rome for inspiration in matters of administration as well as in artefacts and architecture.

Though it was situated in the north, a long way from either Rome or Constantinople, Aachen was far from unsophisticated. The great octagonal chapel built by Charlemagne had a dome over 100 feet from the floor, whose antique columns and capitals had been specially imported across the Alps from Italy. Hot springs at the town enabled Charlemagne to erect baths which rather crudely followed the pattern of the Roman *thermae* – on a far smaller scale.

Administration was centralized and concentrated in the hands of the Emperor and his inner cabinet. The scriptorium at Aachen, under the guidance of the English scholar Alcuin of York, was engaged in the almost insuperable task of transcribing from scroll to codex all of what remained of latin literature. It is probable that three-quarters of known latin writings owe their preservation to the activities of Alcuin and Charlemagne.

The influence of Byzantium was so strong in the ninth century over the whole of the territory governed by Charlemagne that even when, on his death, the empire he created fell apart, the culture of the West was predominantly Byzantine in flavour. So it was not an unknown quantity in the eleventh century when the first crusaders penetrated to Constantinople in the course of getting to Jerusalem.

Byzantium, in the form of Constantinople, was brimming with life and innovation. The streets were clean and the public buildings were constructed of brilliant and polished marble, decorated with mosaics both inside and out. Trees and fountains, splendid dress and military equipment, magnificent soldiers and horses, excited the envious emulation of Europe. The crusaders were astonished by labour-saving devices and mechanical and chemical invention far beyond the West's capabilities. An amazing example was Greek fire, made from a secret formula of naphtha, sulphur, turpentine and pitch. It was ejected at speed out of tubes, igniting when exposed to water on its way to meet its target, usually a Saracen fighting ship. Greek fire was the great terror instrument of eastern Mediterranean war.

The skills of the Greeks were paralleled by those of the Syrians. By the end of the eleventh century, on invading Palestine and Asia Minor, the crusaders met a formidable civilization where, among other things, the arts of metallurgy and alchemy were far advanced.

The faking of precious stones had, since time immemorial, interested the Syrians. The idea of consciously counterfeiting was not in the forefront of their minds. They wished to extend the availability of substances that looked like the exorbitantly expensive precious stones that came from China and India via caravan routes. The combination of alchemy and metallurgy gave them the clue, since the colour in glass is induced through mixing the basic colourless sand and potash with tracings of metal oxides. Different metals give different colours. Thus copper is the source of red *and* green, depending on the chemical composition of the copper salts and the temperature of glass during manufacture. Cobalt produces blue, sodium yellow,(cadmium, unknown as such in the Middle Ages, also produces yellow) and manganese produces a variety of shades from pale lilac and flesh colour to the deepest Tyrian purple. The metal salts change the structure of the glass enabling it to filter different coloured light. Just how this happened chemically and physically was unknown at that time – the formulae came about as a result of empiricism. If something worked it was repeated and possibly refined.

Perhaps the 'noble' names of certain colours in glass and in heraldry are the vestiges of that early and persistent trade in faked gems. 'Ruby', 'emerald' and 'sapphire' are still generic names used in the stained-glass trade.

The Middle Eastern chemist was dependent on sources of supply for his raw ingredients and these could vary or dry up altogether which might explain why particular colours appeared and disappeared from time to time.

It is in the eastern Mediterranean that the ideas of coloured glass, and, as an extension of this, the construction of coloured windows, came to fruition. But they were on a relatively modest and even crabbed scale. Certainly there are references to stained glass in the Arabian Nights tales, written about the time of Haroun al Raschid, the great Caliph of Baghdad and a contemporary of Charlemagne. The results seem not to have been very impressive (unless undertaken by a Genie – in which case we are told the glass was resplendent, brilliant and rich.) The method of fixing glass in the Islamic lands was to insert it into either pierced alabaster screens set in the window embrasure or into cast plaster slabs which received the same treatment. Similar settings can still be seen in some of the rooms of the Alhambra, Granada, Spain.

That there was stained glass in Byzantium has been proved by potsherds found during excavations in Constantinople. Curiously, the colours of the Byzantine remains parallel in a remarkable way those of potsherds of glass from seventh and eighth century windows from Monkwearmouth and Jarrow in Northumberland, England. In both instances the colours are green and blues, not strong, together with browns and a weak purple; not much red was used. This colour range is very similar to that used in the Lindisfarne Gospels, also from that district. There is a certain amount of evidence, in fact, that the artists of the late classical and early medieval times generally

OPPOSITE
Le Mans Cathedral. 12C
romanesque window in
nave

preferred a cool and non-assertive palette in stained glass as in illumination.

From the seventh century onwards there was a fully viable flow of goods from east to west. Haroun al Raschid even sent Charlemagne an elephant as a present, all the way from Baghdad to Aachen. More often than not, though, people were self-sufficient in practically everything except luxuries and therefore it was on portable and personal luxuries that trade tended to concentrate. For the layman the most marvellous things he could admire were personal possessions – weapons, armour, horse trappings, belts, rings, buckles and clasps, all wrought in metal, usually gold, and encrusted with jewels and enamel. Naturally crusaders took home with them artefacts of the Islamic civilization they encountered, spreading their influence far beyond their place of origin.

There were remarkable movements of human beings too, from the seventh to the twelfth centuries. Not only were there recruits from the north of England, and Normans in the personal bodyguard of the Byzantine Emperor, but the habit of appointing bishops across Europe regardless of nationality resulted in Greeks going to England and English bishops being dispatched to Germany and the Mediterranean.

The seventh-century bishop Benet Biscop is credited with introducing Greek studies in the north of England with the result that for some fifty years after his death, the educated inhabitants of the area were able to talk colloquially in classical Greek.

The church, I think, was the main medium for the exchange of ideas. In the early Middle Ages important ecumenical councils brought together churchmen from east and west; later the Church of Rome held further councils, not only in Rome but in other venues in France and Germany. All major councils had experts in attendance and attracted all sorts of talented people – artists, musicians, carvers of ivory, makers of stained glass, architects and others hoping to pick up work; inevitably there was an interchange of ideas.

The institution known as the 'Ad Limina' visit created further opportunity for discussion and cross-pollination of ideas. Every five years each bishop of the Roman Catholic church must still travel to

Poitiers Cathedral, 12C Crucifixion. An archetype of the Christ on the Cross which
is echoed in the great Cimabue Crucifixion in Florence (Photo Painton Cowen)

the Holy See in order to give an account of his diocese. It is an ancient custom and is unbreakable. Certainly the 'Ad Limina' visits were the most obvious opportunity for clients to meet up with bishops and bishops from outlying provinces to make contact with metropolitan ideas – in liturgy and theology, music, art and architecture. The great exchange of ideas was of profound importance in the development of all art forms. After all it is ideas that give rise to art, not usually the other way round.

For the evolution of stained glass the influence of the author known as the Pseudo-Dionysius is of paramount interest. This obscure monk from Constantinople was known only by his pseudonym. Writing in the sixth century, he produced two books which, brief though they were, proved to be highly influential. His two treatises, *The Heavenly Names* and *The Celestial Hierarchies,* which dealt with the composition of heaven and angels, in their ascending degrees of importance, were the inspiration of most theologians in the Middle Ages. From the point of view of the stained-glass artist these two books triggered-off the concept of light being the main constituent, if not the bed-rock, of matter. All was made of light, and the light was the material reflection of the heavenly light, the wisdom of God.

Such was the form of ideas (among many other ideas) circulating round the west during the twelfth century. They were not given definitive shape until the treatises of Robert Grosseteste, Chancellor of Oxford and Bishop of Lincoln, in the middle of the thirteenth century. In his little book *de Luce* (*On Light*) he followed the Pseudo-Dionysius and expounded the idea clearly for the first time that all matter was a question of condensed light. Grosseteste's works were treasured all over Europe throughout the Middle Ages. He wrote over forty books. At the Reformation in England they were totally suppressed and ignored and remained unknown till the middle of the nineteenth century. His theories, founded on a resuscitation of the scientific method for the first time since the collapse of the Roman Empire, anticipated those of Sir Isaac Newton, four hundred years later, with regard to light and the rainbow.

This mention of Grosseteste is perhaps a little premature, but it does set into context just how important the question of light was, as both a philosophical concept and as a trigger towards the disposition and use of light in the new buildings that were arising, first in the twelfth century, and *par excellence* in the thirteenth.

Something should be said here of the concept of 'claritas'. This is a quality of visuality, which, in the Middle Ages, had an importance far from being appreciated today. Imagine a world in which everything was bright and shining and new, a world in which one thing reflected off another in such a way as to enhance the attractiveness and beauty of both – and further, that the visual quality of reflection and transparency was an indication of a higher, moral order, an order which was the beginning of the ultimate reality, which, in a word, reflected heaven. This is the concept of 'claritas' as it was understood in terms of scholastic philosophy of the thirteenth century and probably earlier. It was the most highly prized of medieval visual qualities. The fact that it was largely to be obtained in the physical world by the cross-reflection of highly-polished or metallic objects, polished precious stones and enamel, has little to do with the cult of precious objects in their own right. The main quality sought was one of uplift to the eye and therefore to the spirit, using transparency, translucency and multiple reflection. Though the idea of intrinsic worth was never far from the medieval mind it did not have a central contribution to make towards feelings of gratification resulting from 'claritas'.

The Byzantines had always considered that the eye was the noblest organ of sense in the human body, and that, therefore, the whole visual universe was of the utmost importance in the act of knowing God. This great respect for the eye had its obvious repercussions in the actual practice of Byzantine building. The interiors of the churches were resplendent with the brightest mosaics whose reflections crossed and re-crossed each other in a conscious effort to create a paradigm of heaven. This was fully understood by the man credited with inventing the Gothic style of architecture in the middle of the twelfth century, the Abbot Suger, of the monastery of St Denis, outside Paris. St Denis was considered by some to be Pseudo-Dionysius, and also the Denys who encountered St Paul on the Areopagus, in Athens, as described in the Acts of the Apostles. These beliefs about who the author of the two treatises was, explains why he was taken so seriously.

On the practical plane the evidence for the use of stained glass, and its importance in contributing to the wholeness of the scene in twelfth-century architecture, is to be found in the book *de Diversibus Artibus* by Theophilus, a German monk. This book does not give the impression of being a pioneer effort; it is exceedingly, even inexorably, detailed in a variety of arts and crafts, from ironwork to organbuilding, and includes a large section on the art of making windows. As described, the craft has not changed significantly from that day to this. The processes described in it are those that were already well-known and widely practised. In the sphere of stained glass the small single-figure lights high up in the cathedral church at Augsburg, southern Germany, (which are still in their original position) both date from the period when Theophilus was writing, and demonstrate vividly what he was writing about.

Abbot Suger, when planning to build a new church in honour of the St Denis who had written the books on light and Heaven, was determined that it would, if possible, surpass the visual splendour of Constantinople. He closely questioned the travellers and crusaders returning to France as to exactly *how* big, *how* beautiful, and *how* resplendent, the great church of Haghia Sophia was.

Two factors made his dream a possibility. As well as being influenced heavily by the portable artefacts of the East, such as carpets, the crusaders were highly impressed by the quality of the buildings they saw in Greece and the Near East. It is irrelevant that these were mostly of the fifth and sixth centuries BC; the crusaders had little historical sense. This 'flat-bed' construction, involving the dressing of stone right through the thickness of the wall with little or no mortar between the stones, was a complete reversal of the normal way of building which had up to that time been derived (in a rather inefficient way) from the methods of the Roman Empire. The immediate effect of this reappraisal of techniques was that walls of far greater height and less bulk could be attempted in building without endangering the stability of the structure through overweight and consequent bulge. This revolution in building construction is the basis of all the achievements of the Gothic style.

The second factor that impelled the Gothic was not a technical, or indeed a material factor at all. It was one particular doctrine of the Catholic Church. The doctrine of the 'Communion of Saints' was as old as Christianity itself, but it had particular importance so far as the study of stained glass is concerned. The doctrine was, briefly, that there is an unbroken web of contact and mutual help between those who have died in the favour of God and those, in the Church, who are yet on this earth. This difficult doctrine was of such importance because the intercession of the saints on behalf of those still living meant that a cultus of the saints was a pressing necessity. This fact, together with the Doctrine of the Incarnation, which stated that the Christ, Jesus of Nazareth, was at one and the same time truly man and truly God, fixed the consciousness of western, Christian, art towards the human figure rather than abstraction or geometric non-figuration. And it is on the basis of figuration that all the glass in the Middle Ages, with very few exceptions, was founded. It is a case of 'no cultus of the Saints, no Doctrine of the Incarnation – then no stained glass windows'.

The Gothic was started by Abbot Suger, of this there is no shadow of doubt. With the building of the Abbey of St Denis and its tumultuously acclaimed consecration, a new fashion in church building was initiated. Everyone who came to Paris had to pay a visit to the Abbey of St Denis. The French Crown, whose especial patron St Denis was and whose resting place was in the Abbey vaults, did everything in its power to promote the new style. There was opportunity in France first of all, and then, following French example, in other countries such as England, Germany, the Netherlands and eventually Spain, to expand and play variations on a style that was as flexible as it was original.

For the building of the great cathedrals in the latter half of the twelfth century and the duration of the thirteenth coincided with a period of unparalleled prosperity and expansion in Europe, taken as a whole. What Jean Gimpel in his book *Industrial Revolution of the Middle Ages* has called with accuracy 'the first industrial revolution of Europe' grew and gathered strength. To the increasing availability of money was added the immense proliferation of mechanical and other inventions, the harnessing of water-power for large mills, and the increased use of devices and implements for architectural projects as well as wars. The expansion of men's opportunities was equalled by the expansion of their minds. The growth of the universities in the first half of the thirteenth century is without parallel in any other century.

William Anderson proposed in his book *The Rise of the Gothic* that the aim of civilization is the elimination of fear. At no time is this aphorism more sustainable than in the early Middle Ages. This was largely the work of the Catholic Church. It taught that there was a system, there was a plan and a structure to the whole of the universe in which an infinite worth was given to each and every human being. All the great ecclesiastical monuments of the thirteenth century were built to re-affirm that fact. They generated hope and certainty in mankind. As such they were built out of the conviction of most ordinary people that their lives mattered, that the custodian of their transformation and redemption, the Church, was essentially benign and loving and it was on this conviction that the civilization of the thirteenth century was founded.

The cathedrals of Europe stand out as the greatest achievements of the age. They were not only places of worship, though that was their first and most important function. They housed within their walls the components that we now find split up into various compartments. The roles of art gallery, library, meeting place, morgue, burial chamber, place of entertainment and commercial activity, leisure complex and psychologist's consulting-room were combined within the garth or the interior of the Gothic cathedral.

It could be claimed the cathedral aimed at being the microcosm, a miniaturization, of the great world outside. Cathedrals were built in the conviction that people should, in entering them, be conscious of being on the threshold of heaven itself. They should be aware of being in contact with a life of higher significance, of greater joy, beauty and satisfaction. The very stained glass itself was an integral part of the building, not an after-thought added to the basic structure of the church. Everything that was conceived to be relevant and appropriate for the cathedral was bound together by an all-encompassing conviction that was founded on vision and revelation.

The structures that arose in the thirteenth century were such as had never before been attempted. Giant vaults, so high that an eleven-storey block of flats could be built inside them, were flung over spaces that, in some cases, could accommodate ten or twelve thousand people together. Nearly all have survived eight hundred years.

Nothing, however, was left to chance. We can grasp just how professional medieval architects were by examining the extant drawings of the tower for Strasbourg Cathedral which are still to be seen in the Musée de l'Oeuvre at Strasbourg. The drawings, in ink, on oxhide, dating from the first quarter of the fourteenth century, are of a quality far superior to the architectural drawings that come off most designers' boards today. They have nothing to do with the 'quaintness' that, since the eighteenth century, we have associated with the Middle Ages.

So much for the background and surrounding interests of stained glass. What about the medium itself? It is easy to forget that when it was employed on a large scale, as it first was in St Denis, it was the reproduction in a different medium of arts that had been physically small. That is, the ideas that inspired the stained glass windows, some forty feet in height and ten feet broad, came from illuminated manuscripts and small carved ivories and enamelled reliquaries and the like. All these artefacts were readily transportable – and so the ideas they encompassed could be disseminated throughout Europe with the minimum of delay and impediment. They were shrines of ideas, as it were, that had already stood the test of time. What more natural than to emblazon them on high?

The carvings and statuary which encrusted all the major doorways and piers of Romanesque churches were originally highly coloured and gilt. There are records of fully life-size gilt statues in Anglo-Saxon Britain. All the west fronts of cathedrals were similarly alive with coloured carving in high relief. Accordingly the new expanse of windows was a transparent concomitant to the realistic three-dimensional statues in other parts of the church.

Hitherto, with the close construction of Romanesque architecture, the individual widely spaced, deep-set windows piercing the thick walls afforded a series of separate experiences rather than a generally dispersed *atmospheric* experience. It was as though the viewer went from transparent icon to transparent icon as he progressed up the aisle. Suger, by employing the new flat-bed technique of construction, reduced the interval between the windows and cut down the bulk of the stone-work. Consequently the eye was enabled for the first time to take in a broad sweep of window expanse rather than individual points of interest. This unifying gesture towards not only the windows but also the interaction of the windows with the architecture was the great breakthrough, and on this new formal reality the rest of the achievement of stained glass in the Middle Ages depended.

There seems to be a dividing line between two modes of expression in stained glass following on the great advance of the late twelfth century. On the one hand we have an atmosphere of intense gloom in the medieval cathedral. On the other we experience a dramatic vivification of our senses as we enter, which is quite at variance with the first tradition. The former seems to lower our spirits almost to the point of depression; the latter to raise our psyches to a heightened level of stimulation and awareness. On entering the Stygian gloom of Chartres Cathedral for the first time, according to James Rosser Johnson in his book *The Radiance of Chartres*, the initial reaction of the eye is such as to drive some to the verge of tears, so great is the assault on the fabric of their inner psychological selves. This shock, I believe, was fully intended. The eye is closely linked to the nervous system and the feelings of disorientation and confusion on first entering are in time allowed to give way to feelings of humility and wonder. After four to six minutes of being inside, one's pupils expand to accommodate the gloom, and the result is that an atmosphere of reassurance, rest and joy is perceived to spread evenly throughout the vast building. But the act of humiliation must have taken place first, and this is the mystery of Chartres. To a certain extent the great rose-windows of Notre Dame in Paris, though some ninety years later than Chartres, induce the same kind of reaction.

25

Chartres Cathedral. 12C
south choir clerestory
(Photo Painton Cowen)

OPPOSITE
Chartres Cathedral. 12C
Jesse window at the west
end of the nave, before
cleaning
(Photo Painton Cowen)

Both churches force a reaction on the eye that has the concomitant psychological effect of transforming the memorative and contemplative faculties. In both cases the outside world is forgotten and the world of spiritual transformation begins to take over.

This 'tradition of obscurity' seems to me to be attached to those churches which were primarily pilgrimage centres. The atmosphere was intended to induce feelings of humility and petition in the vicinity of the shrine of martyr or saint. Since the shrine was constantly surrounded by masses of lighted candles (as is the Madonna of Chartres to this day) it was to that focus of attention that the pilgrim tended to be drawn. We must think of the practical reaction between the architecture and the glass and the shrine, with its glowing jewels and flickering candles, as essentially a unity. It was for this that the great church was constructed.

Chartres Cathedral. 12c north rose window, centre (Photo Painton Cowen)

Chartres Cathedral. 12C north rose window, detail with Angel (Photo Painton Cowen)

Canterbury Cathedral. Detail of early 13C window

At Chartres the nave windows are in many ways the most remarkable artefact of the whole building. Very few pieces of glass in their construction are larger than the size of a thumb-nail. The story-telling is almost completely lost in the obscurity of the colour and the multiplicity of the pieces. Yet the overall effect has no parallel in the history of the medium. In these windows in the lower aisles of the church there is a pronounced effect of eastern colouring; the interweaving of the reds and blues recalls that of Bokhara carpets. The nave clerestory windows, rather later than those of the side-aisles, are on an altogether larger scale. This compensates for the distance they are from the eye, for from fifty to sixty feet or more there would simply not be any point in detail. The design, and the actual construction of the glass, were on a broader design-vision.

## The thirteenth century

There seems to have been a crisis in the making of thirteenth-century windows, a crisis of labour. In the twelfth century no labour-intensive work appears to have been avoided, and consequently the intricacy and involutions of stained glass windows from that period in France are truly amazing. The background to the individual historiated panels that make up the window, are of interweaving vines and leaves of the utmost elegance and finesse. During the thirteenth century not only do the individual pieces of glass get considerably bigger but the background fill-in is codified into a straight lattice of red, white and blue. The sheer effort of organization of the myriad separate pieces of glass through the kiln in firing; the trouble taken to get them into their right places once the firing had been completed; the intricacy of the leadwork and the patience needed to assemble the pieces into a coherent design; the enormous extent of the cumulative windows; all this seems to have combined to suggest a broader and more technically immediate solution to subsequent windows at Chartres.

Continuing the theme of 'tradition of obscurity' it is interesting

OPPOSITE
Canterbury Cathedral.
Detail of early 13C
window

35

to take the case of Canterbury Cathedral. This building, having been destroyed on numerous occasions, was definitively rebuilt, initially by Williams of Sens, completed by William the Englishman, soon after the death of Thomas à Becket in 1170. The windows, or what is left of them (a surprising amount considering the peril they were in until the nineteenth century) are of a profound darkness. The quality is extraordinary, far better than the best of Chartres. Much has been said of the blue of Canterbury glass. It is unique, a complete, and most fascinating entity. The unbelievable sapphire of the background burns the eye, and yet it is a radiant balm as well. It is both powerful and an irresistible invitation at the same time. This cushion of transcendental blue acts as a matrix out of which the red and white of the borders gently obtrude. And they in their turn define a space in which the figurative element of the windows plays with the utmost freedom. And what a figuration. The drawing of the individual figures is some of the most precise and vigorous to be found, not only in the Middle Ages but at any time in the history of art. One has to go back to the best spontaneous drawing on Greek vases of the fifth century BC to find comparable examples of such excellence and vitality. For the predicate of this precision and invention is an extreme freedom of handling, an almost throw-away freedom associated today with the development of painting during the time of the Impressionists and after; in fact it is present in any art that has attained the highest state of self-knowledge and self-confidence. In the greatest cycles of Chinese art in the ninth and tenth centuries, and Japanese art in the seventeenth-century, one can see the same phenomenon at play. As in those remote and exotic cultures, so in thirteenth-century Canterbury.

It is possible that one supremely talented master could have painted the complete schema, delegating passages to skilled assistants. This is suggested by a freedom of some of the painting that borders on sloppiness. However, most of the painting is of exceptional quality, the hands and especially the feet being particularly fine. The total unity of expression running through the work is without a blemish.

Canterbury Cathedral.
Detail of early 13c
window

The intention of the Canterbury master was that the story should be thoroughly legible from the floor of the cathedral. The story of the Gospel and the story of the martyrdom were both of intense importance and urgency. The individuality of each separate panel pulls the eye along with all the elegant concision of a good strip-cartoon. The glass panel-cum-picture was created precisely to tell a story, and it would have been thought of as a failure had it not succeeded in this respect. One wonders what kind of brushes the painters used. Laymen, and indeed scholars, are usually unaware how vital the character of the brush is in the formation of style.

Le Mans Cathedral, 13C

If we cross over the channel from Canterbury to the great cathedrals in France we can examine the other main stream of achievement in medieval glass, that of clarity, and of fire. Perhaps we should call it the 'tradition of elevation' lacking any other term, for the effect of glass in this tradition is not so much that of bringing the viewer directly to his knees as of encouraging him to float about for sheer joy. Such churches as Auxerre, Bourges, le Mans and Tours are unbelievably buoyant in the effect they have on those who go inside. These cathedrals are concerned with enabling the person who enters to experience with the utmost immediacy that amazing heightening of the spirit, that integration of the faculties of faith, hope and charity which vivify at a hitherto unexpected level the viewer's very soul. For this effect to work its magic successfully – as it undoubtedly does in all the cathedrals mentioned above – the completest integration of glass and architecture is necessary.

To my mind the choir of le Mans Cathedral is one of the most sophisticated structural conceptions in the history of architecture. The quality of the glass is admirably matched to the economy and elegance of the giant building, with its mouldings over arch and vault, and the extreme attenuation of the columns. Light and structure interpenetrate each other to an amazing extent. It is not possible to appreciate the one without the other, and it seems to me quite obvious that the two were conceived as a unity from the very beginning. The splendour of the colouring at le Mans arises from its extremely high tonal key. There is no area of profound density and consequently the colour sequence follows with breakneck speed. The eye flashes past the sequence almost as implacably as the sequence flashes in front of the eye. A middle-toned blue is balanced and compensated through the use of white and a high scarlet red. The use of brilliant greens is apparent. These, as complements to the red, give yet more energy to the harmonic arrangement of the colour. High celadon greens and emerald are a bold innovation and are widely distributed throughout the ranges of the clerestory. As with Bourges, yet in a far more sophisticated way, in le Mans there is a secondary triforium, as it were, placed over the side-aisle arches, which can be seen through the thinner, taller columns of the nave

Auxerre Cathedral. Plain glazing in 13C retro choir. When introducing light into late 13C churches, the grey-white glass was qualified with elegant non-figurative painting to reduce glare

OPPOSITE ABOVE
Auxerre Cathedral, 13C. Detail of feet

OPPOSITE BELOW
Auxerre Cathedral. Detail of 13C window

arcade. If the eye is allowed to travel from the highest point of light in the nave clerestory downwards it does not reach a point of stasis until it meets the cills of the side-chapel windows which nestle between the elaborately bifurcated flying buttress piers. There are, all in all, about a hundred and twenty feet of coloured glass from vault to floor. The whole complement of windows is of a mid-tone or lighter, and together with a light blue, a rather aquamarine blue, introduced as a counter to the mid-sapphire higher up, makes the choir of the cathedral incandescent with light.

Auxerre should really be considered on its own, but perhaps also as a lead-up to the glory of Bourges. Both are dedicated to St Stephen, the first martyr. As a result both churches are glazed in a red colour

range where red predominates and sets the theme. The net result of Auxerre, whose glass is far from complete and much of which seems to have been switched around the cathedral, is an effect of phosphorescence, sometimes purplish, sometimes greenish, like a giant opal. When you get up close to the glass it comes as a bit of a shock to realize how crude, in fact, the basic colour harmonies are – and indeed the apparent systemization of the colours, for there are only red, white and blue, green and yellow as primaries, together with mauve, lilac, purple, and brown in very minor quantities, as a mitigation of the first colours. The exact reason for the effect of phosphorescence is difficult to analyse; it is something to do with the simultaneous vibration of the different coloured light on the retina of the eye when seen from a distance. But although the effect is easy to determine the exact colour-nature of the experience is very difficult to define in terms of the very thing that brings it about – light.

On the other hand it is impossible to attempt an analysis of Bourges Cathedral. To go into the church, which is unusually built, without transepts and with the nave arcade of immense height, tending to squash the triforium and the clerestory above it into a secondary place, is to enter a flawed design by a singular genius. What is left of its glass, a considerable amount, fills the whole cathedral with a blaze of incandescence. The architecture is the 'Doric' of Gothic, so to speak; it has a rough grandeur, with no fine mouldings or exquisite proportions. Even the method of building is coarse and lumpy when compared with that of le Mans, or Tours, or Sens cathedrals. And yet the glass complements the building almost perfectly – or rather the building shows off the glass to perfection, for it is the glass that triumphs at Bourges. One is caught up into the interior of a burning incendiarism. The reds, repeated and re-repeated, soaring up to the height of the glazed side-aisle triforium, as in le Mans, and invading and overrunning the small chapels that line the circular ambulatory sweeping round the altar, set the tone for an experience far more electrifying than that of Chartres. The effect is that of an explosion of fire-crackers, a controlled and immensely energetic pyrotechnic display. Within the reds

OPPOSITE
Bourges Cathedral. 13C
glazing, apsidal chapel

LEFT
Bourges Cathedral. 13C
ambulatory window,
detail

and spaced out by surprisingly more white than you might expect,
there are areas (connected to the free and mercurial figuration) of
intense grass-green and yellow interpenetrated with blue and brown,
purple and a vivid apple green. The sheer intensity almost makes
one shield one's eyes, especially early in the morning when the sun's
rays are horizontal, and yet this intolerable feast has a spell-binding
effect in that one cannot remove one's eyes from it. The windows at
the bottom of the cathedral are entirely taken up with the serial

depiction of the Gospel story, including the parables and the miracles. It is a good instance of the homiletic basis of most medieval art, where the human figure is concerned. The windows are not so much the Bible of the poor as the proof that there was a vigorous tradition of preaching the Bible to the poor which cried out for illustration as a mnemonic after the sermon.

Generally speaking, as great churches got bigger and bigger, the demand for vast areas of stained glass to be specially designed, made up and delivered on time must have been insupportable. One just has to think of the lower nave windows at Chartres, composed of thousands upon thousands of tiny pieces of glass to be fired and organized, to realize that a change in design procedure was almost inevitable. Backgrounds were simplified; colours were systematized. The design got broader and more bland. For the first time a great deal of glass was white, not only because coloured glass was becoming scarcer and more expensive, but there also arose a new relationship with the rest of the fabric of the building. As cathedrals became ever more enormous and the carvings in the interior began to assume an importance that before had only occurred on the outside, the atmosphere of the building became more buoyant and luminous. Moderating the gorgeousness of the stained glass contributed to this effect.

Amiens Cathedral, designed as one piece by Robert de Luzarches and built between 1220 and 1268 is an example. The colossal undertaking of this cathedral involved enormous amounts of glass for the windows. Though not many of the original ones are left, there is sufficient to see that from the very beginning this church was not designed to be a sacred powerhouse of awe and luminousness. It was a giant assembly-hall for the whole of the populace of Amiens to be present to worship God. There was a spirit of municipal pride in the construction rather far removed from the inspired population of Chartres who gave their labour free to build a shrine to the Blessed Virgin. The glass is eighty per cent clear. Some coloured borders are employed but in general the glass in the west end and round the chevet, and that in the north and south transept rose-windows is the only touch of real colour in the building. As a result, though the proportions are titanic, the atmosphere inside is one of gentle buoyancy and rest and comfort, rather than intense devotion as in Chartres or ecstatic transport as in Bourges and le Mans. We feel very happy and complete in Amiens Cathedral in spite of its size, and surely that was what the architect had intended the effect to be.

One church which dramatically illustrates what has been suggested of the change-over between the new architecture and the old is La Sainte Chapelle in the Palais de Justice, Paris. I proposed earlier that there was an urge to accentuate the devotional angle of a particular pilgrimage or shrine-dedicated church by intensifying the atmosphere in using very dark glass. But the tendency of architecture in the course of the thirteenth century was to evoke feelings of confidence by means of the manipulation of the light inside. An interesting situation arises when, as in the Sainte Chapelle, we find the architecture appropriate to one means of expression being tied in with the stained glass appropriate to another. The anomaly of La Sainte Chapelle is that the glass is very much too heavy and intense for the style of the architecture. This extraordinary structure was built on the command of St Louis, King of France, in order that the relics of the chaplet of thorns which had been placed on the very head of Christ, as was then believed, could be suitably housed for veneration. The chaplet, among other relics, had been bought for an inestimable price from a church in Constantinople; hence the name of the structure, La Chapelle. Though the relics of the chaplet and that of the True Cross were thrown out and burnt at the time of the French Revolution as being uselessly superstitious, the whole atmosphere of this building retains that magical quality which it must have possessed when it was first built. If it were not a museum-piece now, casually shown off by a bored guide (who refuses to close the great doors at the west end, under the later rose window) but still a place of dedicated worship, the effect would be, as it was intended and programmed to be, awe-inspiring. The intense gloom of the earlier cathedrals is here lessened a little; the pressure from the glass is not so overwhelming as in Chartres, for instance. Nevertheless it is of an ancient order and its inescapable intensity seems at odds with the attenuated mid-century style of the architecture.

In the case of La Sainte Chapelle one wonders whether the King, who was paying for the building, insisted that glass of the quality and character of that of Chartres, also paid for by him and his mother, be inserted regardless into a building that was not truly designed to take it. However, this church was a once-and-for-all commission for a unique purpose – it was not an ordinary church or cathedral, and in this special character the justification for it lies.

It would not be right to leave the thirteenth century in France without describing the cathedrals of Beauvais, Tours and Sens. Beauvais is one of a number of unfinished cathedrals which were left over when the drive to construction ran out of steam. There are at least four such buildings in France dating from this period which have never been completed of which Beauvais is the most notable.

One has to come to the present century, perhaps to Cape Kennedy, to understand the extent of the ambition and undertaking which Beauvais Cathedral represented in the consciousness of thirteenth-century France. The vault soars to one hundred and fifty-six feet above one's head as one enters – through the transept, since there is no nave and consequently no west door. The evidence of the threatened collapse of the building some twenty years after the choir was completed strikes one immediately. The choir arcade is reinforced by the insertion of extra columns between the original ones, thus doubling the number. This gives the impression, through multiplication of the verticality, of even greater dimension than in fact the building has. As in Amiens, the glass in the choir has not entirely survived, but there is enough either reconstituted or original, to give one a good idea of what the effect must have been. The same ethereal expansiveness, due to the large amount of white glass, pervades the building, but the feeling is heavily qualified by the necessity of stretching one's neck continually in order to take in the whole structure. The effort, as in a first visit to New York, is apt to bring on headaches and vertigo. Beauvais was built in conscious rivalry to Amiens, and by comparing the two we can have some idea what the architects of Beauvais were after. As in Amiens, the windows high up in the transepts, of a later date than the main body of the cathedral, determine the major sources of colour in Beauvais

Cathedral. There is adequate modern glass round the chevet but it is probably darker and more lush in colouring than the thirteenth-century builders would have envisaged. Nevertheless Beauvais remains an unforgettable experience.

On an altogether smaller scale but in every way more complete than the flawed masterpiece of Beauvais is the cathedral at Tours. The towers at the west end are considerably more recent than the main body of the church, which is later thirteenth century. This cathedral was built with no 'reverse entasis' in the interior. The entases on a Greek column, or across the front of a Greek temple, where the steps of the stylobate gently swell and rise to offset the effects of perspective are familiar. This trimming of pure geometry in favour of perceived reality was known to medieval masons as well; they simply applied the principle to other things. The nave walls, as they rose, were gently inclined outwards until, at the spring-line (from where the vault starts to *spring*) they are a foot or two wider apart than the bases of the nave columns. Tours lacks this refinement and therefore feels vaguely oppressive when one enters. But the glass is of the best late-thirteenth-century period, and is almost totally complete.

There is none of the burning incandescence of Bourges about the choir of Tours, and yet it is a masterpiece. To begin with it is constructed with the 'glazed triforium' principle. That is, the giant clerestory windows, which, taken in themselves, are higher and also more expansive than any others in France, are extended downwards into the outer walls of the triforium. In fact there are no 'outer walls' to the triforium which is totally melded and incorporated, virtually subsumed – into the clerestory.

The glass is a triumph of the integration of a basically simple colour-range, which unfolds and develops into a series of fugues and toccatas, so to speak, translated into visual terms. The result is something not easily forgotten. It lacks the mysterious phosphorescence of Auxerre and the passion of Bourges, but it has a flashing opal fire all of its own and is one of the most vivifying experiences in France. The simple range of colours has not restricted their sophisticated use. One figure in the glazed triforium, for

Tours Cathedral, late 13C
to early 14C, showing
over-ambitious
attenuation in rose
tracery helped by
construction column
raised in the middle

example, has bright green hair, so as to maintain the colour balance and give artistic satisfaction.

Sens Cathedral is another experience entirely. It is one of the earliest to be constructed in France because, as the town was judged to be the most central point in the Europe of the thirteenth century under the spiritual authority of Rome, it was chosen to be the site for major ecclesiastical councils and synods. A conference centre, which still exists, was built later that century.

The sensation on entering Sens Cathedral is one (very like Laon) of gentle serenity and reassurance. This is due to the majority of the glass being of the very early thirteenth century, and employing the lighter, more moderate high-toned blue which was characteristic of the twelfth century. The glass is in prominent frames, geometrically constructed on circles, squares and lozenges, which do not allow the figuration within them to over-trump or interpenetrate them as tends to happen in Bourges. There is a lot of white glass used, and the effect is of a quiet urbanity and peace. The cathedral has an elaborate wrought-iron screen round the choir which was installed in the eighteenth century. This is perfectly suited to the atmosphere already created in the early thirteenth century.

There are too many cathedrals in France to describe them all here, but before we turn back to England for the close of these two centuries we should not omit Laon or Rheims cathedrals. Laon is very early thirteenth century, placed high and inaccessible on a hill all on its own in the middle of the northern French plain. The church is unique in France in having a square east end in the English manner. Originally it was designed to have nine towers, of which only six were completed. The interior, like Sens, does not impose on the viewer in any way. Rather it invites the visitor to feel at ease and restful. The glass is thirteenth century, but again, it is not particularly darkly coloured, relying very much on the colour scheme that was more prevalent in the twelfth century. Blues, whites and greens, and a diminution of the proportion of reds employed makes the interior of Laon buoyant and moderate.

The atmosphere of Rheims, which suffered so much in the war of 1914–1918 is worth noting. The restoration of the whole cathedral

Le Mans Cathedral, mid 13C. The highest degree of sophistication in medieval building craft: choir and coeval glass

was an immense labour spread over many years. The stained glass artist Maître Simon-Rheims was responsible, with members of his family, for the supervision and upkeep of the glass from the 1870s to the 1940s. They seem to have successfully recreated the feeling the cathedral must have had when it was first constructed in the high thirteenth century. Inevitably, much of the glass is reproduction and reconstituted. Rheims provides an opportunity for explaining why, with the intensity and variety of colour used in the windows, there is never a sensation of discomfort in the Gothic cathedral. Owing to halation, that is the individual rays of light continually criss-crossing each other in every direction, the light that the windows cast is commingled before it has the chance (at such distances) to colour the interior with a dappled, or even one-colour, effect. Hence the atmosphere, taken as an entity, is virtually a *reconstituted* atmosphere of the outer, naturally-lit, world. There is no cathedral where this is more successfully and obviously achieved than in Rheims, and it is to Maître Simon-Rheims that we are indebted for such a triumph.

The last example I want to consider from the thirteenth century is from England. In York Minster there is to my mind the most extraordinary phenomenon in glass to be seen anywhere. The so-called Five Sisters window, in the north transept of York is a giant range of five severely simple Early English lancets, all of identical proportions. They are filled with the most magical glass conceivable, yet it is almost entirely without colour.

Whether the idea for an almost non-coloured window originated from the proximity of the three important Cistercian monasteries nearby, Byland, Rievaulx and Fountains, all of them a day's ride away from York itself, is not certain. I am inclined to think that the predominant philosophy of the Cistercians, that of restraint, sobriety, avoidance of statuary and decoration, and no sumptuousness on any account, must have had a considerable influence on the thinking at York – at least in the thirteenth century. There also could have been some cooperation between the workshops that were producing the glazing for the abbey windows at Rievaulx and Fountains and that working on those of the Minster. In fact this is most likely.

Tours Cathedral. 13C
north rose window,
detail (Photo Painton
Cowen)

OPPOSITE
Tours Cathedral. 13C
north rose window,
(Photo Painton Cowen)

Tours Cathedral, late 13c. Detail of choir clerestory windows with plain glazed triforium below, north side

OPPOSITE   Tours Cathedral. General view of the choir clerestory from the south

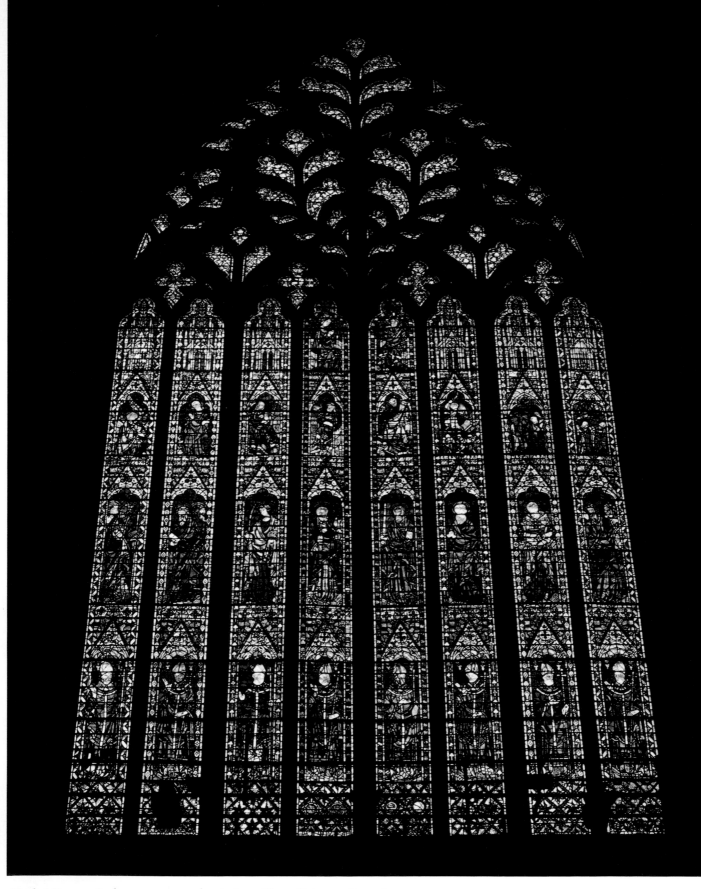

York Minster. Early 15C west end window (Photo Painton Cowen)

OPPOSITE   Sens Cathedral. 14C rose window at end of 13C nave,
seen through the elegant 18C wrought-iron screen to the choir

The windows are in the kind of glass that is known as *grisaille*, i.e. made principally of greys and whites. The Five Sisters are a mazy pattern of inter-weaving white, faint grey, greenish-grey, lighter green-white, warmer whites and horn-colour. There is a hint to me that the idea, if not the actual design, may well have come from a manuscript illuminated in the Lindisfarne or Celtic manner as we can see today in the Lindisfarne Gospels or the Gospels of St Chad, at Lichfield, England. These illuminated manuscripts were far more common – and available for consultation – in the north of England at that time than we can conceive of today. An alternative suggestion is that, before the Jews were hounded out of York, they were very prominent as traders in the city. It is conceivable that there were tissues and cloths from the Near East, Byzantium and Arabia – even India and China – available for scrutiny in York, since the Jews, with their international connections and routes to the East, would have collected such cloths and brought them to the West. Some of these tissues could have survived long after the departure of the Jews in the twelfth century.

Whatever the origin of the Five Sisters, they are unique both for their scale and for the amazingly intricate and sophisticated interweave of colour and pattern they exhibit from top to bottom. There are small points of blue, red, and yellow, with a very occasional dull purple within the maze of ivory and the eye is gently led from one point to the next by this colour and so starts a climb from stage to stage across the surface of the range of windows and so on right up to the very top. The eye can then slowly lower itself using the steadying ropes, as it were, of the lead-line patterns, to effect a safe return to its starting point. All the time the whole window-surface is gently respiring, palpitating, never completely at rest, the various layers of delicately differentiated tones and near-white colours suggesting a tremulous fibrillation which is never obtrusive yet always present. It is this almost sub-liminal stimulus that constitutes the unique quality of the Five Sisters.

Whether the makers of the window projected the effect their work was going to have on those who saw it, we cannot know. It could have been a mere exercise in cost-cutting, as was happening all over Europe at about the same time. But for such a consummate work of art, that theory seems too simplistic. To those who work in the medium it is obvious that nothing in the Five Sisters came about by chance or as a result of artistic naïvety. The makers were artists of a very high order.

# The Fourteenth and Fifteenth Centuries

## *The fourteenth century*

Millennial or centennial marks in the calendar do not change art-movements and there was certainly no great break in the continuity of the western world merely because of the turn of the thirteenth century. All the same there is a significant difference between the feeling of the two centuries. The thirteenth century had all the immediacy and simplicity of a slice of white bread and black-currant jam; the sensation of the fourteenth century in contrast is that of a rich fruit cake.

European civilization was becoming more and more elaborate. There was significantly more money at people's disposal. The universities founded in the thirteenth century were producing an increasing number of people who were prepared to think for themselves. There was more conspicuous display in people's clothing, their small items of personal property, jewelry and so on. Music and song-writing became more intricate, with participants straining over manuscripts as they tried to sight-read the part songs. Poetry abounded, spoken out at recitations, and the newly-devised miracle-plays began to appear, the actions of the characters to some extent mimicking the histrionic gestures of friars in their pulpits.

This shift in consciousness and the awareness that the world was changing very rapidly had its effect on the art of stained glass. The transcendental feeling of the great thirteenth-century cathedrals, where all was immovable and reliable, gave way to feelings of immanence.

There was a new realization of the possibilities of invention and initiative in life. People started looking for themselves – and discovered themselves. The life of Jesus was seen to be enfolded within the brackets of a normal day's experience. This was not to deny or detract from the status of the Incarnate God, but to begin to grasp his reality within the day-to-day common touch of our banal existence. The tradition of storytelling persisted. Take the instance of the *Canterbury Tales* by Geoffrey Chaucer, in which even the lowest of the low were capable of telling graphic tales. Anybody who could invent or tell a story in a novel way was sure of a hearing.

The evolution of a more humanistic way of life in the Europe of the fourteenth century had an effect on what was said in stained glass and on the way it was made. Design in general follows the same pattern of development. This is as obvious in the evolution of medieval architecture as, today, it is in the development of the car or of aircraft. Stained glass is an accoutrement of architecture, and therefore its relationship with the main design-concepts of building as they evolve is of great interest. As mentioned in the previous chapter, towards the end of the thirteenth century there was a movement away from the excessively heavy colouring of the beginning of the century.

This change-over is neatly demonstrated if we take the example of the Abbey church of St Pierre at Chartres, a large building at the bottom of the hill behind the cathedral, near the River Eure. St Pierre comes as a surprise. For a start very nearly all the glass is original and in its correct place. The church has a full complement of windows. Towards the choir, however, there are two or three bays of tall clerestory windows on either side of the church. These have been glazed alternately with figurative glass telling gospel stories, and plain glazing, all except the border. These bays are precisely the ones that would have been above the choirstalls of the community of monks. The tall windows round the chevet are in heavily coloured glass, to reduce the impact of the early morning sun. The same arrangement is found at Chartres Cathedral, up above.

St Pierre can teach us some interesting things. At first glance we notice the severe schematicization of the colour. This restricted palette is in total contrast to the marvellously spread-out palette of some fifty years before. Then, in the first two decades of the thirteenth century, the elaboration of the designs and their intricacy seemed to call for a spring-like palette, several greens, red and blue, yellow, pink, purple, mauve, brown, and a great variety of whites. But in the early fourteenth century, there is a distinct tinge of autumn about the colouring, deep red, white and a severe blue, together with yellow, brown, dull pink and a deep sap green. It is obvious that a certain amount of economy came into so restricted a colour range, this being an abbey church and not a royally endowed cathedral, but the proportions of the colours are worked out with sensitivity, and the flow of the design round the church is unified and curiously satisfactory. We are witness to the beginning of a new aesthetic style in glass.

The subject-matter of the windows was of great importance. There is a series of scenes from the Gospel proceeding right round the church. Large single figures, as would have been usual high up in the clerestory, are avoided. The scale of the stories is easy enough to read from the floor. The liveliness of the scenes, however, indicates a further development. That is, the designs are beginning to be influenced by the spectacle of the miracle-plays that were beginning to be written about this time. The figures have an animation and a vocabulary of histrionic gesture that seem to be taken from the plays.

These were, after all, a new expressive medium then, very much as the movies were in the 1920s. Other arts found it impossible to escape their influence. The scenes from the beheading of St John the Baptist include Salome doing a deep back-bend in front of King Herod.

The character of the figurative drawing in fourteenth-century-glass takes on a self-conscious air, rather like a fashion-plate. It is all style. Figures posture and prance. They strike attitudes, some of them outrageous, and engage in gestures towards one another with an air of arch affectation. But then it was an age of luxury and over-exaggerated elegance: the arches of Westminster Palace had already, in the late thirteenth century, been altered and heightened to accommodate the steeple head-dresses of the court ladies.

The new slickness with the brush seems to have pervaded the whole of Europe, from York to Bohemia. Grey and white mincing bishops danced their way through Europe's stained glass windows. The drawing was highly artificial and amusing but dubiously devotional or religious.

Signs of further economy can be seen. Since only the figures, as the objects of attention in the window, had to be coloured, everything else could be executed with a saving in mind. The backgrounds, the borders, the increasingly prevalent architectural details in the design, could all be rendered in white glass – or with the minimum of colour incorporated into them. The art of painting on glass came into its own as a necessary part of the whole design rather than, as hitherto, a mere qualification of the individual piece of glass. The eye was drawn across the window surface by the painting being able to leap across the lead rather than being encapsulated within the leaded outline surrounding the glass.

As the designing of architecture and glass was more and more interlocked, we find the architectural device of the canopy over the figure's head becoming ever more important in stained glass. Aesthetically this helped to give prominence to the main figures or scenes, since they were in colour, and the canopy-work above and pedestal below were in plain white glass, heavily painted. The three-dimensional canopies above the carved figures standing in their niches of carved masonry were reproduced in the design of the glass, the one art truly echoing the other.

The light allowed in through the windows, so crudely dealt with in St Pierre, is, as the century progresses, spread out over the whole range of windows in a church so that a perfectly even greyish light begins to qualify the interior. At Rouen Cathedral the lady chapel is filled with delicate greyish quarries in glass, against which the figures, of rather secondary importance, stand or kneel. The light steals around the figures and into the body of the church in a gentle, lambent luminosity. The quality of the glass, and of most glass at this mid-fourteenth-century period, has a pearly grey quietness.

The predominantly grey and white format was qualified by being stained in part. The 'silver stain', which varies from the most delicate daffodil colour to that of rich amber, was a discovery of the four-teenth century. It probably originated in Germany where there was an intense interest in chemistry and practical experimentation in scientific matters. The staining of the glass suggests to me a side-effect accidently discovered by alchemical practitioners in Germany. If silver oxide or silver nitrate is spread or painted (in solution of water and gum) onto the glass, and even if the glass is rubbed with pure silver, when it is heated in a stained-glass kiln (to about 600°C) a change comes about in the ions surrounding the nucleus of the glass molecule. The scale of intensity exhibited by the stain does not only depend on the strength of the silver solution. It is also affected by the actual chemical make-up of the glass which receives the stain. This makes the process of staining unpredictable even to this day. But when the new technique was distributed across Europe it very rapidly became a favourite device for obtaining yellows, far brighter and more sensitive than those hitherto produced by the use of sodium to colour the glass *all the way through*.

A new aesthetic sprang up from the invention of silver stain. Instead of unifying by means of blues, as we have seen in some of the French cathedrals, or by red, as in other instances, the possibility now arose of unifying the whole extent of the window by means of gold. The use of stain for this effect became enormously popular throughout Europe. Certainly Germany, which had always had a preference for unifying by means of yellow, was to employ stain for the rest of time. The generic name for the medium, 'stained glass' dates from that period.

England was not long in adopting the medium of stain. The provision of white light is always a necessity in northern churches and we witness the use of very light-toned glass in the choir and extreme west window in York Minster. All the details that can benefit from a sprinkling of stain receive it, with the result that most of the stained glass in York Minster, and in the surrounding parish churches, from the middle of the fourteenth century onwards, has this added embellishment. The rather dark fourteenth-century nave windows have a surprising amount of white glass in their construc-tion, but it is doubtful whether stain was used there.

York Minster. The schematized serried ranks of saints in the west end window (Photo Painton Cowen)

OPPOSITE
St Pierre, Chartres. Early 14C apsidal window before restoration

Gloucester Cathedral.
The 14C Crécy window,
detail

RIGHT
Zouche Chapel, York
Minster. Quarry of bird
frightened by a spider, 14C
(Photo Painton Cowen)

The greatest example of the use of stain in England is in Gloucester Cathedral. The window commemorating the great English victory over the French at Crécy was inserted, during the later fourteenth century, into a structure of startling novelty.

The choir of the cathedral had been altered some twenty years before in order to accommodate the pilgrims flocking to the tomb of Edward II, popularly deemed a martyr. The old Norman nave had been reduced to the barest bones of masonry, and on these and between them, were constructed a fine filigree of perpendicular Gothic tracery. The vault rose to more than seventy feet in a complicated and subdivided system of vaulting ribs. At the end of the church is the largest window in England, some forty feet in width and seventy in height. This is filled with the most impressive glass in the royal colours of red, white and blue, together with a very great number of details in yellow stain. Most of the window is made of white glass but the painting and the staining sprinkled over the entire surface rings so many changes that the eye is never tired – nor exhausted. The bottom figures are mostly white with staining for the colour of their hair; further up, the canopy-work above the figures is finished with crockets etched out in silver stain. The drawing is extraordinarily fine, firm and precise. It shows great verve and imagination.

France was not in any way behind in the aesthetic adventure of the fourteenth century. It is easy to forget that, with all her problems of politics and the wavering fortunes of the French Crown, France was immensely, colossally, rich. The incursions of war might have been humiliating and frustrating but they did not have much effect on the growth and continued prosperity of the French economy. The amount of money available for art did not appreciably diminish. It merely tended to be placed in directions other than cathedrals. Unfortunately there are very few extant examples of secular glass in France.

The secular aspect of stained glass in England could be imagined from the remains of the building by John of Gaunt at Kenilworth Castle, Warwickshire. John's great banqueting hall, which is now a virtual ruin (as a result of bombardment in the Civil War of 1648)

THE BEAUTY OF STAINED GLASS

still has sufficient large and commodious windows to suggest that there was a good deal or armorial and other decorative glass in the building. Certainly that great achievement of medieval building, the Great Hall at Westminster which was built in the late fourteenth century by Richard II, is notably lacking in windows. But since the walls were far older, they are not penetrated by the fashionable wide fourteenth-century windows, only remodelled thirteenth- or even twelfth-century ones. In the Netherlands, Germany and Bohemia the fashion for erecting large secular buildings forged ahead. Here again the windows were not entirely filled with dense coloured glass, but there was an increasing concern for the beauty and prestige inherent in armorial glass, giving style and status to a building.

If Gloucester Cathedral is the most exciting from the point of view of stained glass, Ely is by far the most original structure in medieval England. True, the enormous octagon that spans the nave is entirely in wood but the ingenuity of the whole construction of eight converging cone-shaped vaults meeting in an octagonal band at the top is an original masterpiece. *From this* a smaller lantern octagon protrudes, now filled with Victorian stained glass of reasonable quality, but in the fourteenth century it must have been filled with finely adjusted coloured glass. The site and feeling of the structure demands such a refinement.

The most beautiful indication of French stained glass of the fourteenth century is in Normandy and thereabouts. Rouen, the capital of Normandy, was eighty per cent destroyed in the 1939–45 war. It is the repository of some really beautiful glass, most of which, owing to timely removal, has survived. We have already seen the effect of the lady chapel glass in Rouen Cathedral, but it is by inspecting the glass of the church of St Ouen nearby that we see the fourteenth-century style of stained glass at its best. This great church was John Ruskin's favourite Gothic monument, and it certainly has a completeness (being built, as Amiens Cathedral, all in one style and at one time) which is not usual in the Middle Ages. The glass and the architecture seem to be in complete harmony with one another, the design of the two together being of enormous sophistication. The windows are just coloured enough to give a sense of fullness

Ely Cathedral. The early 14C vaulting of the lantern, looking up

LEFT
St Ouen, Rouen. Details of clerestory windows

Evreux Cathedral. 14C
and 15C glass in apsidal
chapel

and maturity in themselves but they are not overstressed so as to upset, by drawing attention to themselves too much, the delicate balance between the glass and the wonder of the intricate architecture. The interior effect is made up of a series of delicately modulated greys and off-whites, to which the understatement of the glass is a vital contribution.

In Evreux Cathedral the windows in the side chapels and the high clerestory windows of the chancel are the epitome of all that is good and attractive in French fourteenth-century glass. The smaller panels of richly coloured glass let into the windows are of great interest. In many cases their colour is highly self-conscious. It is almost as though the panels are small transparent paintings in glass that happen to be hung where they are. There is an element of haphazard caprice in their placing, although the general scheme of interval between plain glass and coloured panels is reasonably regular. The great glory of Evreux Cathedral, however, is the series of windows at the end of the lady chapel. The three behind the altar were presumably inserted to tie in with the design of the shrine to the Blessed Virgin, actually sited on the altar, since the very centremost window, at the back of the Virgin's statue, is filled with less interesting glass. The other two windows, on either side, are of the fourteenth to fifteenth century and are quite singular in the quality and sophistication of their rich colour harmonies of blue, green, yellow, and mulberry. They are one of the most important monuments of the Middle Ages.

A major factor in the development of western art was the transference of the Papacy from Rome to the French town of Avignon, on the Rhône, between 1307 and 1377. Without the Papacy Italy was no longer the hub of Europe. Whatever she accomplished during this period lost its pan-European impact. Her activity in painting and sculpture was of little international interest; even though the seeds of the Renaissance might have been sown, they were dormant. Northern Europe, particularly France and England, without Italy's powerful influence, was able to enjoy an originality and confidence in its own judgement that it was not going to regain until the early eighteenth century. The age of what has subsequently been labelled the 'International Gothic' style had arrived.

A contributory factor in establishing this new style was the continuous intercommunication between the various parts of Europe, and the marriages between the royal families and the leading houses of Europe. A more homogeneous culture resulted, influencing artistic practice. The styles of illumination, for example, became more uniform affecting the drawing in stained glass.

Everyone who *was* any one spoke elegant French. French part-singers were in demand all over Europe and French jesters made a living everywhere. The Pope himself, at Avignon, was French more often than not. It was a time when the all-pervasive influence in art was that of the slightly rubbery-textured flowing garments, spriggy trees, tight little bushes and a multitude of animals, fox, rabbit and hind among them, that we find above all in the tapestries of the period.

The career of the Duc de Berri set the tone of achievement in the closing years of the fourteenth century so far as art was concerned. He was the builder of many things. Twelve of the castles he built are commemorated in the *Très Riches Heures du Duc de Berri*, commissioned by him but not completed in his lifetime. The Duc de Berri was insanely extravagant, in spite of having a sharp little shrew of a wife who might have restrained him. The Duc d'Anjou, his brother, and the Duc d'Orléans were also immoderate. The grand tapestry of the Apocalypse, originally about a hundred and fifty yards in length and thirty feet in height, commissioned by the Duc d'Anjou, still hangs in the castle at Angers.

Much of the French royal princes' extravagance was financed by Italian, mainly Florentine, bankers. They could only look on at the spectacle because they were debarred from behaving in the same manner by their social status in society. However the French example had been set and the Florentine resolve towards conspicuous display was firmly rooted. It was to be the factor that would wrest the role of arbiter in the arts away from France for two hundred years.

The art of stained glass has a noticeable habit of taking its stimulus from other arts that happen to be flourishing at the same time. In the twelfth century it was the influence of enamels and illuminated manuscripts; in the thirteenth sculpture; in the fourteenth sculpture

Evreux Cathedral, apsidal chapel

Evreux Cathedral, Lady
Chapel, 15C

and architecture; in the late fourteenth and the fifteenth century the influence on stained glass was mostly that of tapestry. Nevertheless nothing changed in a perceptibly drastic way. The series of windows round the ambulatory at Bourges Cathedral dates from the early fifteenth century, and the easy flowing naturalism of much of the subject-matter in them shows the influence of drawing these was equally at home in a tapestry cartoon or a stained glass cartoon.

The most beautiful window in the Bourges ambulatory was donated by the then richest man in the world, Jacques Coeur, whose motto was '*Aux Coeurs Vaillangs Rien d'Impossible*'. Its subject is the Annunciation and the style is of a gentle naturalism, almost of an illusionism. This contrasts strongly with the intensely mannered style that was typical of much fourteenth-century art.

## The fifteenth century

Naturalism was the hall-mark of the fifteenth century. It is seen fully developed in the dainty freshness of the miniatures of Jehan Fouquet, native of Tours, in his exquisite illuminations in a group of superb manuscripts. However he was not alone. The general trend toward keenly observed naturalism is seen in the *Très Riches Heures*, illuminated from 1409 to 1416 by the Limbourg brothers. This preternatural scrutiny, the sharpened eye, had its origin in the Low Countries. The brothers van Eyk are said to have invented oil painting. In fact they utilized a technique that had been known for centuries and practised in a coarse way on stone and woodwork. By exercising judgment and refinement the van Eyks transferred this commonplace builders' method to small wooden panels and raised it to the highest plane of achievement in the process.

The fame of this startling illusionism in panel-painting quickly spread abroad – along the trade-routes, in fact. The most important axis of trade running through Europe at that time was connected to the wool and cloth industries. There was a line of production running from Yorkshire and the Pennines in northern England south through

80

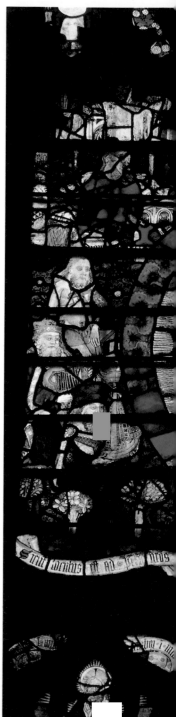

**OPPOSITE**
Rouen Cathedral. Lady
Chapel windows in
*grisaille* (grey) quarries,
14C

**ABOVE**
Great Malvern Priory.
15C windows in
ambulatory, The Seven
Days of Creation, detail

**LEFT**
Great Malvern Priory.
15C transept window, the
Assumption of the Blessed
Virgin Mary, detail

Ipswich and Colchester to the great spinning and weaving towns of Flanders and on into the cloth-dyeing and finishing-mills of Tuscany. Most of the entrepreneurial work and organization was dominated by the Italians. They were at the same time the sources of credit and of commercial security.

As a consequence of the close links in the Netherlands between the artists who designed tapestry, those in illumination, and others involved in the design and production of stained glass, this naturalism influenced the design of stained glass at an early stage. But the activity and development of naturalism in painting had a bearing on people's expectations in the other arts; particularly was this so in tapestry. It is difficult to over-estimate the number of tapestry compositions that left the looms of Flanders and northern France in those days. The industry was so widely spread, employed so many people, spinners, dyers, weavers, finishers, cartoonists, researchers of stories, spinners of special-effect silver and gold thread and so on, that tapestry can almost be compared with the film industry today. It gave a very similar service to the public.

In the greatest houses the tapestries were apt to be regularly changed, as we now look for a change of film. When the great feudal lord progressed through the countryside from one castle to another, his personal retinue was proceeded by the furnishers and the cooks travelling on ahead to prepare the abandoned carcass of the castle to receive, with decorum and comfort, the portentious retinue when it arrived. Fires were lit, beds assembled and made, tapestries were hung in all the principal rooms and meals were prepared. The echoing shell was habitable once more. The Duc de Berri had twelve castles to choose from; the Duc d'Orléans had as many, and they paled into insignificance when compared to the Duc de Bourgogne, the grandest of them all, a petty king in all but name.

This intense activity in tapestry did one great disservice to stained glass. The naturalistic approach to drawing, both of the human figure and of the emergent landscape views behind, tended to contrast too violently with the canopy-work framing the scene. Canopy-work was really a left-over from the previous century. The question arose as to why to tolerate a straightened convention in one direction if

Bourges Cathedral. 15c Jacques Coeur's Annunciation window (Photo Painton Cowen)

85

artists were breaking with such things in every other direction? There was a dichotomy between the niches and crockets of the fifteenth-century architect and the tradition of wide and fluid landscapes and figure-compositions that truly were more appropriate in tapestry or in illuminated manuscripts.

The history of stained glass in the fifteenth century is almost a history of the escape from an architectural straight-jacket. The first victim of change in glass was the border. Borders are important to glass in much the same way as mouldings are to architecture. They act as a periferal 'buffer-zone' between glass and architecture and avoid a direct confrontation between what could be two quite disparate art-forms. Suppress the function of the border and you risk declaring war between stained glass and architecture.

There were mitigating circumstances. In most specific cases of art judgment in the Middle Ages the eye was arbiter. Although there was a distinct loss of architectural cohesion in the design of windows, particularly towards the latter part of the fifteenth century, the stained glass is still very beautiful to look at. Sufficient attention was paid to tonal values throughout the composition, whether it was executed in painting, tapestry or stained glass, and there was not too violent a 'push-pull' effect such as occurs when the tonal values of a painting are too highly contrasted between dark and light. In stained glass windows, when the informal approach is fully exploited the results do remind one uncannily of transparent tapestries. There may be nothing wrong in having a glittering tapestry-like composition hanging in the window-frame, but it *is* radically different from the rather straightened architectural discipline of previous success in window design.

There was a parallel expansion in technical matters to match the new vision. Technique is nothing when considered in isolation and to invest technique with authority is a modern fallacy. If something is deemed necessary and beneficial, technical means will be found to provide it. The situation arose where the Flemings (they were the first) invented landscape painting, and everyone wished to copy such a bright idea in other, perhaps less appropriate, media. The accurate rendering of landscape in glass is difficult. The question of aerial perspective arises. How is the blueness of the receding landscape to be accurately expressed in stained glass, especially when it is rather difficult to achieve in painting? Atmospheric perspective and the progressive diminution of human figures in perspective had both to be introduced into the stained glass repertoire of possibilities. Accordingly a staining blue was invented. That is, a blue (usually of an ash-blue tint) was manufactured that would be capable of taking a stain. The stain, as on white glass hitherto, could vary from a deep amber to a delicate daffodil colour. The effect of stain on blue is to turn the blue to green, and it does not need very much imagination to foresee that great use would be made of this technical possibility in the creation of naturalistic landscapes. We find stained blue glass all over France, Germany and England in the course of the fifteenth century. The effect is undoubtedly very beautiful. On the blue, which perhaps (through sensitive selection of the original glass) varied from light blue in the background to heavy blue in the foreground, the scenes were painted, large in the foreground, miniature in the background. The front of the scene was stained with various strengths of silver stain, the different combinations becoming more and more naturalistic in their representations of foliage and grass and the like. The background could be left with the faintest veil of paint, and indeterminate detail, on the original pale grey-blue, and would suggest, with great accuracy, the effect of a receding landscape, as in painting.

Although there was a great drive towards naturalism in glass in the fifteenth century there was an almost equally strong surge in armorial, heraldic art. The great achievements in this *genre* waited until now. The repeat element in heraldic art, with escutcheon piling up on escutcheon, together with mantling and crests, made for a brilliant decorative effect. The bold colours in heraldry were still highly attractive, and the escutcheons themselves tended to become more and more subdivided, thus increasing their decorative potentialities. The sharp divisions of colour into red, blue, white, yellow, purple and green that we find in heraldic art were still very much in the nature of stained glass.

The continuing influence of the mystery play is evident in English stained glass of this period. The small but perfectly formed series of creation windows at Malvern Priory, in the west of England, could almost be seen as the frames from a film of the creation. God the Father is in deep earnest as he goes through the necessary motions to get the stars to rights, and his six days of labours have the theatrical immediacy of the scenes from mystery or miracle plays. The details are exquisitely drawn and the painting in general is as good as anything in an illuminated manuscript. The hand which was capable of painting this glass was surely equally up to illuminating manuscripts. In spite of guild rules to the contrary, this could easily have happened.

One of the greatest centres of activity in stained glass during the fifteenth century was York in England. The great east window of the Minster, behind the retrochoir, is divided into many little scenes depicting the Gospel story, and each one is a perfect composition. The figures are disposed of in exactly the same way as figures in a mystery play. This comparison is no fancy, since there were well-known and well-attended mystery and miracle play-cycles in York, and in cities such as Wakefield, Chester and doubtless many other northern towns. Had some texts not been destroyed during the Reformation period we should know much more about them. Much of the basis for conceiving figurative art at this time in England was based on the knowledge and experience of plays. This activity gave impetus to stained glass.

In the fifteenth century the designs of German glass began to move towards a smallness of scale and intimacy of execution. It was a period when the idea of private patronage of glass panels, usually of armorials, became more and more popular. The ingenuity of the nation which perfected the clock and the hand-pistol, invented printing by means of movable type and had very nearly a monopoly on scientific instrument manufacture at that time, came equally to bear on the problem of exactitude and finesse in painting on glass. A close scrutiny of German fifteenth-century glass leaves one with the feeling of ones own lack of skill. The dexterity of the brushwork and the use of the steel needle and the sharpened quill in scraffito-work is incomparable. During this period the alchemists were at work as ever and we begin to suspect the invention and use of very strong acids such as *aqua fortis* and *aqua regia*. Acids would enable practitioners to etch glass away, thus exposing the white under-layer below the green, red or blue over-film when the glass was made by a layered technique, as it sometimes had to be. The use of a wax resist would have occurred to glass-painters since it was used in the later years of the century for etching techniques on metal.

By the end of the fifteenth century the pressure for the minute delicacy demanded by small-scale armorial panels suggested new techniques. By grinding away a thin layer of coloured glass to expose the thicker white base-glass it was possible to effect the change of colour necessary to make the quarterings on the armorials. At first only red and green could be worked in this fashion, but soon the range increased. The thinner glass was usually at the back of the finished piece, so as to give a free unimpeded surface which could be painted or stained. The paint was also used to crispen up any areas which were ragged and untidy as a result of using the grinder too sloppily.

Techniques for enamelling on glass were also developed. Coloured glass was ground down to a powder, then mixed with a fluxing agent and a little gum and applied to the surface of the glass. This was afterwards fired at a carefully controlled temperature in much the same way that stain had been in the past, that is, at a temperature which was some thirty degrees lower than that used in the firing of painted glass.

The Italians were, curiously enough, never very good at stained glass, which remained a poor cousin of painting. They did not understand about colour in glass in the way that the French, the Flemings and the English did. It tended to be too sweet and suffocating. Moreover there is an *ad hoc* indeterminacy about the general design of the lead-work with the lines flowing all over the place and joining one another awkwardly – not having a balance and a harmony that is apparent everywhere in France and England.

Florence Cathedral's giant dome was the first to be built since that of Hagia Sophia in Constantinople a thousand years before. The round windows in its drum needed stained glass and Florentine artists, such as Ghiberti, Donatello, Ghirlandaio and Andrea del Castagno were commissioned. The results have the appearance of an enhanced fresco, with a freshness of colour which escapes the narrow range associated with armorial glass. The avoidance of the 'jewelled' approach in favour of larger, broader areas of colour lying next to one another or interpenetrating only minimally is a phenomenon that will not be seen again until the mid-twentieth century. This optical discipline, which was found in Italy as a result of the painting of so many frescoes, of conducting the eye across a broad field of one colour to pass it on towards another colour, was not sufficiently exploited at the time when it was (presumably accidentally) discovered. It remained for Jacques Villon and Marc Chagall to resuscitate this phenomenon in glass in our century. But then we must remember that they, as the Florentines before them, were primarily painters, and it is the painter's eye, disregarding commonplace craft solutions, that, in favourable circumstances, can ring a real change in stained glass and make people see the medium afresh.

The bright spring of fifteenth-century Florentine glass was not to be prolonged. After all it was the product of that interim period when the categories of Gothic and Renaissance had not been defined. The intangible transition from the one to the other exercised no censorship on the arts. Consequently that particular aesthetic which is associated with mid-fifteenth-century stained glass in Italy had only a brief life, before it was overtaken and eventually suppressed in the overwhelming enthusiasm for the true principles of the Ancient Roman style urged by the supporters of the great theorist and practitioner Leon Battista Alberti.

# The Sixteenth to Eighteenth Centuries

## *The sixteenth century*

It was one of the disappointments of nineteenth-century scholarship that, in its enthusiasm for everything medieval, it totally neglected the achievements in stained glass of the three centuries separating the fifteenth from its own.

Although there was a continuation of the fifteenth-century Gothic idiom well into the Renaissance period in northern Europe there was a vigorous restatement of the medium in Renaissance forms.

It is not uncommon for two or more styles to run almost in harness at certain periods in history. The early sixteenth century was no exception. In stained glass we find the older tradition of Gothic running parallel with the newer ideas of Renaissance glass. Sometimes windows of both styles appeared side by side, as in Vendôme, France. Sometimes the styles were combined, perhaps bizarrely, as in St Etienne, the parish church (not cathedral) of Beauvais, France. The justly famous window of St Etienne is almost the last kick of the Gothic, although it was finished well into the sixteenth century and contains portraits of Francis I and Henri II as ancestors of Christ! Technically this window is one of the most remarkable products of the high Gothic tradition that has come down to us.

The colour of the Renaissance windows in general remains that of the heightened realism of the previous age, but anything that in the least way touched on architecture and its derivatives was totally changed. This had a decisive effect on the sense of space and the linear composition of the window. In fifteenth-century stained glass the verticals were heavily qualified, whereas now, although they

La Sainte Chapelle, Paris.
Early 16C rose window
(Photo Painton Cowen)

were still there with a vengeance, a balance was struck in the composition between vertical and horizontal similar to that which is found in painting. The eye, instead of tending to trace from cill to apex of the arch, was equally at home traversing from side to side. The embrasures of the windows helped in this since they were no longer, for the most part, closely set mullions all parallel to one another, only occasionally tied together visually by the crossing of the transoms. Cusping and traceries, those details of design that cut the plain windows of Gothic into a hundred odd ogival shapes in the head of the window, had by the sixteenth century largely disappeared – except in Spain, which was lagging almost a hundred years behind. The last Gothic-style cathedral, not a partial cathedral but a whole one complete to the last detail, was finished, in Spain, in the late 1580s. Then the style lapses almost entirely during the seventeenth and eighteenth centuries except in Bohemia and Oxford.

In Paris the greatest and the most curious – almost grotesque – churches of the sixteenth century are St Eustache and St Etienne du Mont. The great church of St Eustache, near les Halles, is an almost incredible restatement of the Gothic cathedral, in all its majestic proportions, but three hundred years too late. The glass of the mid-sixteenth century to seventeenth century had a compulsion to employ all the 'architecture within architecture' devices of the late Gothic, but this time the design makes use of a perspective which is little attached in concept to the actual body of the architecture. The windows at St Eustache show all the ingenuity of the period, but they are colourless and lifeless compared with those of a hundred years before. The actual idiom of the church in the interior, is of a stilted and wire-drawn classical character which does not actually express anything apart from a yearning to be able to combine the best of the proportions of the thirteenth century with the most up-to-date Roman classicism. However, when the failure in this respect is conceded, the interior of St Eustache (whose building coincided with the destruction of every great monastery in England) remains a magnificent monument on a giant scale of the eccentric and the eclectic.

Eccentricity is the hallmark of St Etienne du Mont, overtowering

Paris on the south bank. This church represents the dying embers of the Gothic, slightly earlier than St Eustache. It has the most original features including a jubé or choir screen of staggering complexity and instability. Nearly all the glass is younger by half a century than the architecture. I suspect that the scheme of glazing was originally intended to be far more vivid and incandescent than it has turned out to be. But the extraordinary themes of the windows and their highly original format marks them as a milestone in glass. The best of them (that is, the worst of them) dates from the seventeenth century and puts one in mind of the little books of emblems, complex images with hidden meanings, which were published all over Italy and France at that time. The theme of Christ as the wine-press of God seems eerily reminiscent of the tortures casually inflicted on antipathetic prisoners at that time which are shown in the *Orbis Pictus*, the first fully illustrated latin primer of the early seventeenth century, by Isaac Comenius.

The Roman Catholic Church was hardly in any position to challenge the secular developments of culture in the sixteenth century, since it had been ripped asunder by the suicide of the Reformation and rendered practically impotent in the north of Europe. Any statements of real conviction regarding ecclesiastical culture had to wait until the era of post-Reformation self-confidence re-emerged towards the end of the sixteenth century. The end of the fifteenth and beginning of the sixteenth centuries saw the rise of nationalism in western Europe. From being a loose confederation of principalities, all holding roughly the same political ideals, Europe became the continent of separately identified nations that we know today. The spectacular growth of secular building coincided with this definition of nationhood which was bound up with the consolidation of the concept of a fixed and firm monarchy in every country outside Italy. The establishment of a court entailed a fixed venue for works of art, as distinct from that of the last century when the great feudal magnate journeyed across the country from castle to castle.

Francis I set the pace in France, as Henry VIII pioneered a new style in England. The series of palaces and giant Tourainois châteaux erected by Francis I in the first half of the sixteenth century finally

La Sainte Chapelle, Paris. Early 16C rose window (Photo Painton Cowen)

95

turned civilized minds away from the draughty, hastily-assembled, ménages associated with later feudalism. Walls were covered with tapestries or the newly-woven crimson damask and cut velvets from Genoa in Italy. Occasionally there were the more exotic and infinitely more costly hangings of Spanish leather. These consisted of whole hides which, after having been embossed in elaborate repetitive patterns usually associated with flowers and still-life compositions, were painted and gilt. Large paintings, framed in gilt-encrusted sculpted wood, were hung on the damask. They came from Italy – Venice or Rome or Florence. The floors were of exquisite wooden inlay, highly polished. White glass, in pieces as large and flawless as could be obtained, substituted in the windows for the crabbed and bubbly tinted glass set in narrow lead calms that had hitherto been accepted. It was a case of an entire transformation of decor which did not bode well for the art of stained glass. After all it was virtually impossible to have the picture-content in the oil paintings, so recently hung for the first time, in flagrant competition with the same type of content in the windows. Glass which had painting and coloured images on it would have inhibited the light coming into the halls and anterooms and the atmosphere would have become overcharged.

But if the idea of stained glass receded beyond recall in respect of the secular decoration of the sixteenth century, it was not so in some churches. The southern French cathedral of Auch is a case in point. The architecture belongs uniquely to the Gothic. The choir seems to have been finished first and entailed the building of a series of giant windows of the most phantasmagorical design round the ambulatory. Each window is about forty foot high and there are at least twenty of them. Taken together these windows are one of the most extraordinary achievements of the sixteenth century in western Europe, so far as stained glass is concerned. At first glance they do not seem to be French in origin, since it is very difficult to connect their design and layout with any of the painting going on at that time – between 1510 and 1530 – but it is easier to see a parallel between this heroically designed glass and the style of painting that obtained about fifty years before in Venice and the Lombardy plain. The style brings to mind the Vivarini and Crivelli, not to say Car-

paccio and Perugino, in the flourish of banners and attitude of the figures, or painters of the Ferrarese school such as Cosimo Tura. This would have been possible bearing in mind the ready cross-fertilization of talent that could occur. After all, even in the sixteenth century, appointments to episcopal sees were still liable to be made throughout Europe which cut through national barriers. Matteo Bandello, the famous author, was appointed bishop of the See of Agen by Henri II in 1550 – and he was from Lombardy in Italy. Agen is only some thirty miles from Auch.

In Auch Cathedral there seems to be a marked discrepancy between the disciplined design in the actual lights of the windows and the wildly inflated surrealistic character of the crowning tracery lights. The latter seem to belong to some fantastic marginal decoration of an illuminated manuscript rather than to stained glass

LEFT
Le Mans Cathedral. Early 16C north transept rose window

RIGHT
Tours Cathedral. The 16C flamboyant rose above the west end, restored by Max Ingrands in the 20C

proper, and yet they must have been conceived when the stonework of the windows was designed and erected, because the unity of traceries and the windows fit together perfectly.

In Alsace, which almost seems to have escaped both the Reformation and the Renaissance, the glass of Metz Cathedral is well worth some scrutiny. It seems extraordinary to me that a structure of great elegance dating from the thirteenth century should not be furnished with thirteenth-century glass throughout. But then we learn that the cathedral is a marriage between two disparate churches and has a sixteenth-century apse of a 'faked up' thirteenth-century style, entirely filled with sixteenth-century glass of a very high order. The general lightness of the church is heavily qualified by the dark lushness of the choir glass, in which the hottest rubies and the most resonant blues clash vibrantly, only kept in discipline by the interposition of marvellous golden colours produced by the use of stain on an extended scale. The small ambulatory round the apse provides an opportunity for examining the sixteenth-century glass at close quarters, since it is very probable that it was designed by the same hand as the windows a hundred and thirty feet above our heads. In the southern of the shallow transepts there is a large window, not altogether successful, which rises to the full height of the church. This is in a very definite classical style, in actual fact later than the glass in the choir, and it makes no attempt at Gothic nostalgia.

It is not surprising that the stained glass in Flanders, relying as it did on cartoons similar in style, scale and disposition to those of the tapestry workshops, should have attained full architectural and figurative maturity in the Renaissance manner sooner than any other northern centre.

The enormous window designed by Bernard van Orley in the Cathedral of Ste Gudule and St Michel, Brussels, is a kind of apotheosis of the marriage of Mary Hungary and Louis II Jagellon of Poland. The use of the architectural background as an airy triumphal arch, a *trompe l'oeil* in fact, with steep perspective and marvellously foreshortened figure-perspective is one of many vastly ambitious schemes of stained glass that we can still see in Belgium, all of them dating from the first half of the sixteenth century. The architecture could well have been an inspiration for Alfred Stevens' Wellington memorial in St Paul's Cathedral, London.

The later sixteenth-century Gothic architecture of Spain is for the most part, singularly deficient in windows. The greatest of the cathedrals, those of Salamanca and Segovia, hardly have any glass to speak of. Seville Cathedral, built a hundred years before, is an exception, the glass being very fully coloured; it was inserted into the fabric of the cathedral almost into the eighteenth century.

After the enormous destruction in the churches of England at the time of the Reformation, there was understandably little call for new stained glass. The windows of the great chapel at King's College, Cambridge, continued to be slowly filled as the schemes of design for the glass progressed from ante-chapel towards the altar, but apart from this, all other glass was imported from the Netherlands in small quantities for use in private chapels. This had to be on a very modest scale, avoiding 'Popish' subject-matter.

There was one marvellous break, however, and that was the inexplicable revival of chivalry and mimic medievalism during the 1580s. The great hall of Gilling Castle, built by the Fairfax family in the later sixteenth century, has the best-preserved collection of armorial glass for its date in England. The style is very like the Flemish of the same date, with its strap-work cartouches and Germanic flourishes. The armorials themselves, with their multiple quarterings, are not as fine, taken individually, as those of the contemporary German or Flemish escutcheons, though they are of a high order.

Armorials are on the whole underestimated. Most viewers merely survey the general results, and through ignorance miss the real achievement. There is a great diversity in the actual painting of armorials, especially in the sixteenth- and seventeenth-century examples, for they display a subtle amalgam of the strictly heraldic and the naturalistic. The compressed devices or 'charges', as they are properly called, are drawn and painted with deadly precision and economy but without forfeiting the life and energy inherent in natural subjects – such as animals, birds and plants. These have a surprising vitality and a wide-awake quality which only becomes apparent if the viewer takes the trouble to examine the escutcheon closely. In looking at the charges attentively and sympathetically we begin to realize that these tiny objects are the lineal descendants of the flourishes and grotesques and incidental idiosyncracies that, in the Middle Ages, were found in the borders of illuminated manuscripts. Some seem to have lifted qualities from the Walt Disney character of those delicious fourteenth-century drawings found on the quarries of the Zouche Chapel in York Minster.

One of the most accessible ranges of windows from sixteenth-century Flanders is to be found in Lichfield Cathedral's lady chapel where a series of enormous windows were glazed early in the nineteenth century with glass from the Abbey of Herckenrode, near Liège. This abbey was the victim of dissolution in Napoleonic times. Just how beautiful the latest of medieval glass can be is demonstrated here – I say late medieval although the idiom is Renaissance. Mrs Jameson, in her book *Legends of Monastic Orders*, suggests that the designs are by Lambert Lombard, 'the first, and by far the best, of the Italianized Flemish school of the sixteenth century.' Whoever designed them, the use of startling red in concatination with greens and a strong stain is a formula for the most spectacular sixteenth-century glass in England.

## The seventeenth century

Whereas the sixteenth century can be viewed as the tail-end of the Middle Ages, the seventeenth century was wholly devoted to a new style, only very rarely looking to the past. The full-scale conviction of Renaissance classicism, and its derivative, 'baroque' was overwhelming. It precluded any attachment to images frozen into the embrasures of a window such as were associated with the northern aesthetic of stained glass. That was condemned as of barbaric or 'Gothic' taste, hence the birth of the term, originally one of disdain.

Where coloured light *was* employed it was under the presupposition that a theatrical effect was desirable. This demonstrates once again the propensity of stained glass to take cues from whatever art was in the ascendancy at any particular time. The seventeenth century was *par excellence* the age of theatre. When any age is the subject of upheaval in politics or social life, the ground is fertile for dramatic invention. This was so from the age of Pericles onwards and never was it more evident than in England during the Elizabethan and Stuart periods. Theatre in England had its contemporary parallels in Spain and France and Italy. The use of glass in the proper sense during the baroque period was minimal. Even a great all-round artist like Bernini had the sensibility of a competent plumber when it came to realizing the potentialities of glass. The embarrassing crudity of his lighting effects on the set-piece of the *Ecstacy of St Teresa*, in Sta Maria della Vittoria, Rome, is little more than a theatrical light, with a yellow filter, shining down on the sculptural masterpiece. The same goes for the gigantic *Altar of the Chair* at the end of St Peter's, Rome, where the Holy Ghost, in the form of a white dove, amid a strung racket of crudely radiating rays, spreads its benediction through the employment of a brassy yellow in the giant oval frame set high above, beyond Bernini's sculpture. Such was the nadir of 'stained glass' in seventeenth-century Rome.

The influence of the baroque, stemming from Rome, was nowhere more evident than in the churches erected by the Jesuits all over the continent of Europe from Cadiz to Crackow. Antwerp had its full complement of these baroque churches since there had been a thorough rebuilding programme following the total desecration of Catholic places of worship in the town by gangs of Calvinists in the latter years of the sixteenth century. Apart from the cathedral, there was no Gothic ecclesiastical edifice left in the city. The enthusiastic adoption of the baroque in Catholic Flanders may partially explain the curious and delightful phenomenon of the recrudescence of stained glass in Calvinist Holland early in the seventeenth century. One has an idea that the emphasis on stained glass may well have been a reaction to the new-fangled style, the baroque, in Flanders.

There was not much theatre in Calvinist Holland, but there were an awful lot of tiles being produced at Delft and other centres in the seventeenth century. It is not surprising that here the pervading influence of the tile-maker had as much effect on the style and form, and indeed technical possibilities of stained glass as ever the art of the tapestry-weaver had some two hundred years previously. The art of filling a window with coloured glass patterns and pictures (for that is really what they were) entailed the division of the glass into a series of straight-sided quarries, inevitably white, on which the subject was drawn in black paint. The black paint was fired first, which left the glass free to be overpainted with transparent enamels in a wide range of colours – which could be further modified by stain. Where really saturated colour was required – as in the robes of figures which might have to be in red or blue – the straight colour was employed for the drapery, and leaded out separately from the quarries.

The finest achievement in this technique is at the great Gothic church at Gouda in Holland, where four giant windows from floor to ceiling are glazed fully with elaborate historiated pictures of a very high quality. I cannot say more than that since I was rudely denied entry by a custodian who had just closed the door of the church, and with characteristic Dutch stubbornness refused me the view of it 'even for a moment'. However the skills of the stained glass craftsman came to England from Holland at that time in the form of the van Linge family, who glazed many a window in Oxford in the early seventeenth century, when it was under the benign and 'popishly-suspect' rule of Archbishop Laud. It is possible to see many examples of the van Linges' work in University College, Lincoln College, the cathedral of Christchurch and other places in Oxford, and this Dutch work can be studied from quite a short distance, adding to the pleasure of seeing the rather lumpy imagery in all its ingenuity. It all has a pleasantly 'cobbled together' provinciality about it, owing nothing to the major art movement of the day but an achievement in its own right.

While the art of stained glass was carried on in a small but endearing way in Caroline Oxford, the great windows of King's College Chapel, Cambridge, continued to be slowly filled with historiated glass, much of it from the Low Countries.

St Etienne, Beauvais. Mid 16C Jesse window, detail

OPPOSITE
La Trinité, Vendôme. 16C
renaissance window

LEFT ABOVE AND BELOW
St Etienne du Mont, Paris.
Details of 17C stained
glass window

RIGHT ABOVE AND
BELOW
Auch Cathedral. Part of
an extensive range of 16C
windows in chapels round
the apse

OPPOSITE
King's College Chapel,
Cambridge. Christ
releasing souls from Hell,
by Bernard Flowers
(Photo Painton Cowen)

OVERLEAF LEFT AND
RIGHT
Lichfield Cathedral Lady
Chapel, Flemish 16C
classical glass from
Herckenrode Abbey,
Liège, installed 1802

New College Chapel, Oxford. The Jervais/Sir Joshua Reynolds window in the antechapel, mid 18c  (Photo Painton Cowen)

## The eighteenth century

The power of the painted image in the late-seventeenth and eighteenth centuries continued to dominate all related image-based art. Since painting employed subtle changes of tone and dissolutions of outline – was firmly attached to visual appearances in fact – and since these desired effects would be best obtained by the subtlety of glazes and scumbles in oil-painting technique, the arts that were not oil-based found it hard going to keep up. Porcelain painting and tile painting, within their own tight disciplines, were immune from the distortion that one form of art suffers if it tries too hard to emulate the form and expression of another. Not so tapestry and stained glass. The beautiful tapestries issuing from the looms of Beauvais and the Gobelins were shamelessly copying all the traits of the great painters of the time. Indeed the genre-painter Jean-Baptiste Oudry and that consummate genius of design, the painter François Boucher, were successively directors of the French royal tapestry works of the Gobelins. Their influence was paramount in turning the whole expression of tapestry down the ultimately blind alley of copying paintings. The great tapestries were more akin to large-scale scene-painting and indeed in their proper location they did 'set the scene' for many a social occasion. Then, as now, the French authorities were most supportive of an art-activity with potential for export, and the aggrandizement of French prestige ensued. Tapestry and porcelain were exported in quantity in the eighteenth century bringing not only revenue to France but the additional kudos of being considered the most cultured nation on earth.

So far as stained glass was concerned, this spin-off did not occur. The desire for imagery in *windows* had completely evaporated with the emphasis on imagery on the *walls* of the great public buildings. The thin and desultry elegance of the glass in Versailles Chapel gives us the clue as to just how far the eighteenth century in France was prepared to go. It was a mere stutter of motifs, as in a high-class frame round a picture – only in the case of the chapel there was no picture to be contained. Elsewhere, as in Besançon, the windows that eighteenth-century bishops inserted into a venerable thirteenth-century choir resemble the quality and design of Savonnerie carpets more than anything else. One is left with the impression that, like children in Victorian times, the stained glass of Louis XV was to be seen and not heard; it was never allowed to preponderate and claim any merit on its own account.

However, throughout the eighteenth century, England still retained some nostalgia for stained glass, partly because of a streak of eccentricity running through the English character, and partly because at any one time in the history of English art there is never the extreme dismissiveness accorded to past modes of expression as occurs in France. This may be a puzzle for those who have formed an impression of the wholesale destruction of glass in the Reformation period, but we have to remember the prominence in English consciousness of sixteenth- and seventeenth-century antiquaries and historical savants such as John Leland, John Aubrey, Elias Ashmole and Sir Thomas Dugdale. These great men focussed attention on the remains and ruins of medieval England, if not its values, some two hundred years before the French conceived such an idea. As a result, the English, although emancipated from the ethos of the Middle Ages by the new mental climate of the Reformation, were more open to acquiring knowledge about medievalism than the French who dismissed it with contempt.

Nevertheless, the successes in stained glass in England during the eighteenth century remain pretty meagre. Most of them are to be found in Oxford. There is a rather neglected window in the chapel at Oriel College, which demonstrates the difficulties of treating glass merely as a kind of transparent fresco. The series of windows by Peckett and Price in the respectively left-hand and right-hand sides of the choir of New College, Oxford, deserve special attention. Those by William Peckett have a refulgent innocence, not to say naïvety about them. They have what Sir John Betjeman called a 'Bright Pavilions' quality. The actual designs are said to be Italian, with Peckett being the executor of the work and collecting the credit. This seems very probable to me since there is a distinct stylistic parallel between what we see in the windows and the slightly sinister designs of the eighteenth-century Italian Tarot cards, which took on their present-day definitive form in that century. A great deal of enamel is employed, including a high light blue, and there is much stain. The figures look like giant cut-outs from a nineteenth-century Pollock's *penny-plain twopence-coloured* theatre set.

Opposite Peckett is the very much more sophisticated art of William Price. The single figures in niches are beautifully posed, owing something, I suspect, to the influence of Sir James Thornhill, England's only truly indigenous baroque painter. Their stances and gestures are not empty and grandiloquent. There is a nervous energy and urgency about them and a reality about the anxiety of the expressions on the faces, a great care in the richness of the harmony in the colour-schemes, that brings this range of windows into a category all of its own. Not that William Price was immune to the pervasive influence of painting, since there is a heavy chiaroscuro which is hardly appropriate in the medium of stained glass, but this is handled with very great sensitivity. The great west window of Westminster Abbey was also the work of Price; it was designed by Sir James Thornhill himself. The cartoons for the designs of the single figures feature in the 'Marriage à la Mode' painting series of William Hogarth, who was Sir James Thornhill's son-in-law. The cartoons are at present hanging in Chinnor Church, Buckinghamshire, England, and are full-scale oil-paintings.

Whether artists who were interested in, or who wanted to reconstruct, the Middle Ages at this time were influenced by the theatre is difficult to determine, though it is probable. Where would the experience of the Middle Ages come so vividly to mind except in the plays of Shakespeare, above all the historical ones. The interplay of deep shadow and highest light, of darkest vice and clearest purity, is put forth in an altogether unforgettable way in his plays. It seems likely to me that people's concepts of the Middle Ages were formed by seeing plays about the medieval kings of England, and for these to be effective, the employment of dramatic chiaroscuro by footlights and candles was essential, hence the dramatized light and shade of Price's art.

In the antechapel of New College there is one of the most controversial and vilified windows in the history of art. I refer to the

'Reynolds' Window', for that is what it is called, irrespective of its subject-matter. The centre window of the antechapel is a more or less straight rendering of an oil-painting cartoon by Sir Joshua Reynolds.

Unlike the earlier Peckett and Price windows in the chapel proper, Sir Joshua's window reverts to the seventeenth-century Dutch mode, that of dividing the whole window up into evenly-measured quarries of white glass on which the subject-matter is painted in transparent enamels (or at any rate as transparent as they could be at that time) pushing the dramatic effects of light and shade to their ultimate. The maker of the window was Jervais of London, and it is said that when the finished work was exhibited in the capital, prior to being installed in Oxford, everybody was astonished and delighted. But then in London it had been exhibited under the best possible conditions, as a famous picture might have been shown. It was in isolation; the walls of the exhibition room were draped in black; there was no back-light coming from unforeseen sources to blank-out the image partially or distract the viewer's attention.

Jervais must indeed have had a difficult job to make anything of the cartoon at all. The colours were entirely of the bistre, van-Dyck-brown, ochre and burnt-Sienna range – something of startling novelty in glass even now. There were occasional areas of dull grey, pink and shafts of brilliant stained golden colour. The canopy-work above the heads of the subsidiary figures to either side of the main subject, the birth of the Saviour in the stable, was particularly unconvincing. It has not the slightest vestige of true medieval conviction about it.

However, the window was eventually inserted – to universal horror. It still stands out like a sore thumb, upsetting the tenor of the antechapel with an eighteenth-century heavy confidence which pushes aside the vastly more sensitive and moderate fifteenth-century glass in the other windows.

Nevertheless something must be advanced for its justification. Like another gross intrusion into Gothic completeness, Narciso Tomé's *Transparente* in the ambulatory of Toledo Cathedral in Spain, Reynolds' window is best seen at a particular time of the

Narcisó Tomé. Spanish, 18C. Section of the *Transparente*, Toledo Cathedral

day, under particular conditions, and only when these are fulfilled does the window begin to justify itself. Tomé conceived the vastly more complicated and significant *Transparente* to be seen early in the morning, between 6 and 8 a.m.; only then does it make sense and give the overwhelming experience intended. Reynolds' window, whether conceived as such or not, really ought to be seen at the opposite end of the day. It seems to have been designed as a grand *coup-de-théâtre* on the congregation coming out of the choir after evensong – say between 5 and 7 in the afternoon. The coming-out time coincided with sun setting directly behind the window. The organ-screen of the chapel prevents the full impact of the window; meanwhile its golden glow spreads a suffusion of light through the narrow opening of the doors under the organ loft which can be sensed as you sit in the choir-stalls. When the congregation has left the stalls and is processing far down the aisle the scene in all its golden and daguerrotype glory bursts upon them, flooding their minds with the reassurance of the birth of the Incarnate Word. It is in this theatrical context, rather than in a straight role as 'autonomous art-object' – as we subconsciously tend to categorize all art nowadays – that we should view the Reynolds' Window. It was saved from, if not destruction, certainly permanent removal, in the interests of 'good taste', at the end of the 1939–45 war by the vigorous intervention of Sir John Betjeman.

The end of the eighteenth century in England saw the emergence of an increasing sensitivity towards the possibilities of stained glass, largely as the result of the eccentricities of Horace Walpole and his followers who cultivated their version of (grossly inaccurate) 'Gothick' in the teeth of fashionable, Ionic, opposition. Early 'Gothick' stained glass was very well behaved and ever so dainty – in fact it was a good deal too dainty – but even this effete affectation of art had its influence in nudging the sensibilities of the *cognoscenti* towards the *possibility* of entertaining 'Gothick' ideas. What started out as play and self-indulgence, matured eventually into serious study and careful measurement, the subvention of all true achievement in architecture. The Gothic Revival could be said to have begun in the drawing-rooms of the aesthetes.

# The Nineteenth Century

The progress of the Gothic Revival is easy to plot, through the end of the eighteenth century and the beginning of the nineteenth, but its precise origins are difficult to define. There seems to have been, in the beginning, a dichotomy between the boiling, inner turmoil of mind that found expression in the 'Sturm und Drang' romanticism of Goethe's novel *Werther* in the 1770s, and the very external conformism of the Neo-Classical art movement (c 1765–1825). This psychological tension and pressure was to find a European outlet in Napoleon's campaigns – so much so that by 1815–17 the conviction behind the Neo-Classic movement was running at very low pressure in favour of a romantic preoccupation with the Middle Ages. The Gothic Revival had come of age by the 1820s. It started out as a literary fad fostered by Sir Walter Scott in Great Britain and by Châteaubriand in France but gradually it took hold and was accepted everywhere. Initially the architecture was pursued with more passion than discretion; proportions, details, emphases and decoration were unsure of themselves; architects made mistakes, misjudgements.

Eventually, however, a formidable amount of accurate and dependable scholarship accumulated entirely due to the close inspection, and measurement, of the monuments of Gothic building that had been neglected for so long. The exact details of mouldings, for example, were measured, and the fall of light on them and its effect was registered and appreciated.

If architecture was foremost in expressing ideas of the Middle Ages, stained glass was not too far behind. In England the restoration of Windsor Castle as a viable royal residence was undertaken by Sir Thomas Wyatville. It is unlikely that the expenses for this under-

Ely Cathedral. 19C nave window in 12C opening. An early reconstituted idea of 12C glass by Thomas Willement. Pinball colouring.

taking would have been paid by the English Parliament had it not been seen as a constitutional reposte to the forces of Imperialism on the continent, and Republicanism across the Atlantic. Both these political movements were heavily associated with the neo-classical modes of the late eighteenth century. Henceforth, except by certain powerful Whig families, the neo-classical style was abandoned in England.

A powerful combination of imagination and this political atmosphere enabled the revival of stained glass to forge ahead in England. At first there were fairly feeble efforts by such artists as Francis Edgington. In time, however, the true principles of the medium were studied and noted; serious efforts were made to colour glass in the manner (as it was then understood) of the medieval masters. By the 1830s, sufficient information about the design of medieval stained glass had been gathered to enable such powerful designers as William Warrington to distinguish between the various historical periods of the Middle Ages. He was able to produce, *ad lib*, the style required by the architect. Warrington was equally at home with the Early English style, the Decorated and Perpendicular; for his armorials he even referred back as far as the sixteenth century. In all his designs he was enormously painstaking and accurate. However, the results inevitably do have a strong tinge of early Victorian pedanticism about them.

The Romanesque style, or 'Norman' as it was dubbed, Warrington tended to leave to other hands. Principal among these was Thomas Willement whose spectacular and brilliant windows for the south aisle of Ely Cathedral are almost unbelievable. They remind one of a series of dazzling pin-table machines with different colour-combinations. At the time of their installation they must indeed have caused a sensation. More than a hundred years later, in the 1950s, when public opinion of Victorian stained glass had reached its nadir, there were those who wanted the windows taken out – and presumably destroyed. Once again it fell to Sir John Betjeman to prevail on the cathedral authorities not to remove them.

In some respects Willement stands as a unique artist of 'pop' stained glass a century before its time. He was in part emulated by

LEFT
St Andrew, Trent, Dorset.
Three-light window by
Arthur O'Connor, 1871
(Photo Painton Cowen)

RIGHT
Waterford, Hertfordshire.
Two Angels with the
Ascended Christ, by Sir
Edward Burne-Jones,
*c*.1896 (Photo Painton
Cowen)

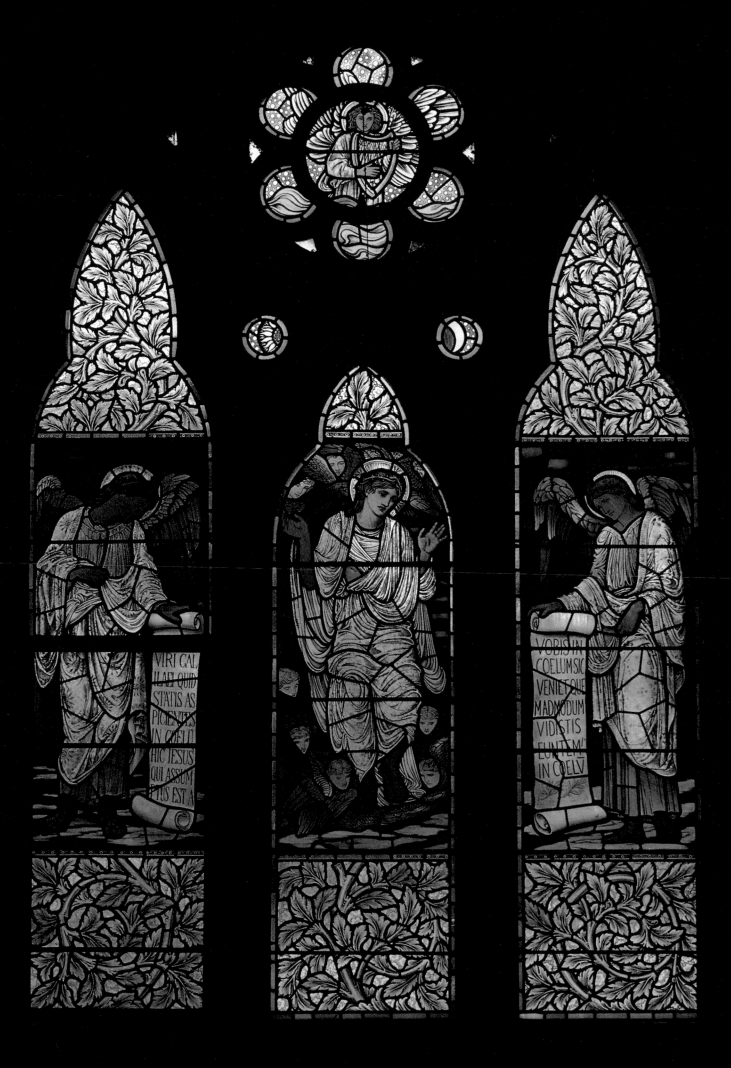

Paris 'Belle Epoque'. Au
Printemps department
store (Photo Painton
Cowen)

RIGHT
Caisse d'épargnes, Nancy.
Commercial Art
Nouveau, 1880s–90s
(Photo Painton Cowen)

Arthur O'Connor whose sense of colour was very much better, but whose sense of drama and colour-combination was almost over the top. One does not forget an O'Connor window. His technical virtuosity in managing to assemble the myriads of tiny pieces employed in his windows is amazing. The colour has a Celtic intensity and lushness most unusual in nineteenth-century glass.

Enormous firms were required to cater for the heavy demand of a movement with such breadth and scope as the Gothic Revival. There were many varieties of style and different designs were employed on every conceivable occasion. The largest firm in England in the mid-nineteenth century, Messrs Clayton and Bell, claimed to be able to make 'a window a day, and two on Sunday'. The firm John H. Hardman and Sons, still in practice today, undertook all the stained-glass commissions given to them by A. W. Pugin, the Gothic and ecclesiastical architect. Pugin, whose father was a French émigré from the Napoleonic *débâcle* of the Ancien Régime, is reckoned to have done a hundred years' work in only thirty. The intense effort of incessantly, and accurately, drawing church after church, building after building, country house after country house, undertaking the while the entire decorative scheme for the new Houses of Parliament (designed by Charles Barry) eventually drove him mad. The whole concept of the Houses of Parliament covered thirteen acres of ground beside the Thames, and every detail, both inside and out, from the weather-vanes on the top of the tower to Big Ben, every moulding, nook and cranny, panel, crocket and cusp, down to the very soap-holders in the gentlemen's lavatories, were designed personally by Pugin. Nor was stained glass absent – Pugin designed the whole of that too. It was fifteenth-century in style and highly successful.

M. Jean Lafond, surely one of the most authoritative scholars of stained glass, in the course of a speech to the British Society of Master Glass-Painters in the early 1960s, claimed that the greatest period of creative art in English stained glass was the nineteenth century. I do not think he was wrong. A stupendous amount was produced in the course of the years between 1815 and 1914. The first efforts in the medium were almost inevitably unsatisfactory from the colour point of view. But then art is often the victim of the prime sources of material available, and almost the only tints to be found up to the 1830s were the relatively mass-produced ones of the heraldic range – crude red, blue, green and white, together with the occasional hot and fiery stained yellow and a lush purple. Then a series of experiments regarding the making of glass and the pioneering of colour were carried out which eventually enabled what was approximately the range found in medieval times to be produced. In this respect England owes much to the experiments and careful formulae noted down by Charles Winston in the middle of the century. Without Winston's patient enquiry, which was published in the 1860s, it is doubtful whether the true subtlety that we find in nineteenth-century English glass colour would have existed. The French command over colour lagged a long way behind Great Britain at this time for precisely the reason that Winston's researches were not available to them in translation.

As well as great architects who chose deliberately to work exclusively in Gothic, such as Giles Gilbert Scott, George Street, James Pearson, William Burges and the like, there were talented men who, while not tied to the Gothic idiom, knew all about it, could practise it at will, but who really tried to pioneer an individual personal style to which the Gothic contributed. William Butterfield was just such. His brand of Gothic never really approached anything that had been built in medieval times; it had a similar relationship to Gothic proper as the range of Renaissance architecture from 1415 in Italy had to the Roman Classical a thousand years before. Each was a legitimate exfoliation and development of what had preceded it. Each realized certain potentialities that had lain dormant in the style. This explains the originality of Butterfield. He was not alone in this since before his day the much underrated English architect Anthony Salvin had erected some astonishing buildings in the 1830s and 40s which range from the thirteenth-century pastiche, Peckforton Castle in Cheshire, to the astonishing extravaganza involving the Elizabethan, Jacobean and Louis XV styles, known as Harlaxton Manor, outside Grantham. Alfred Waterhouse, too, was a surprisingly innovative architect, combining all styles outside the Gothic together into his own idiom. His designs for the Museum of Natural History in South Kensington, London, involved some of the most beautiful coloured architectural drawings of the period, and his revolutionary design for University College Hospital, London, is still impressive.

The foundation of the Ecclesiological Society, which gave advice on just such items involving matters of liturgy and church ordering – things that the clergy were not so sure about – and its predecessor, the Camden Society, meant that there were, up and down the country, a growing corpus of clergy and enlightened laymen ready to listen to architects and adopt their suggestions.

By the time of the Great Exhibition of 1851, the production of stained glass had enormously increased. Inside the giant Crystal Palace at Hyde Park there was an extensive gallery of stained glass available for sale by the yard at prices to suit every pocket. But the design of stained glass had ceased to be an exotic novelty by this time and had become subject to stringent aesthetic criteria. On the standards laid down by the *cognoscenti* in the 1860s, most material exhibited at the Great Exhibition would not have passed muster. The inaccurate, or perhaps too painfully accurate, plagiarizing of medieval models was seen to be out of harmony with the fresh ideas seemingly spontaneously arising in architecture and painting. Something more than a mere dull repetition of the past, however justified in its accuracy, was called for in the new Victorianism of the 1860s and 70s.

Two movements in the world of art in England, not unconnected with each other, performed the task of bringing the ideas of Victorian stained glass to their maturity. In the 1850s the Pre-Raphaelite movement urged painters to get back to the hard-edged and visually uncompromising art that the protagonists, William Morris, Edward Burne-Jones and William Holman Hunt, associated with the art of Italy before the advent of Raphael – hence the name of the movement. The painters of the Pre-Raphaelite movement were not confined solely to their easels; they branched out into the decorative arts as well. The designing of ceramics, tile-work, stuffs, wallpaper and stained glass were looked upon as a logical and desirable extension of their studio activity. None was more adept at this than William

Morris. He was a designer rather than a painter, but his association with painters and his early efforts as a painter meant that his eye had been trained in the visual discipline of picture making. As a consequence everything that he produced had a visual integrity – so much so that his designs persist in use today with no suggestion of tiredness or exhaustion. His famous dictum 'only tolerate in your house what you know to be useful and what you believe to be beautiful' rang through the upper echelons of Victorian society like a call to arms; it is still valid today.

The later, less tightly defined movement known as the 'Aesthetic Movement' flowed in part out of the previous one. By the 1880s there was a feeling that the resources of Europe were not fertile enough, not original enough, to be able to give expression to the amazing diversity of life that had arisen as a result of the activities of the nineteenth century. The revolution in transport, resulting from steam engines in trains and boats, meant that artefacts could be brought with speed direct from India, China and, above all, Japan. It was the impact of far eastern art, especially that of Japan, which changed the character of much stained glass, freeing it from the purely ecclesiastic, and changing the ideas as to what could or could not be designed and arranged in stained-glass panels. Secular stained glass on a serious scale could be said to have begun with the new emancipation arising out of the Aesthetic Movement.

What we witness as we contemplate the movements in art and architecture of the 1870s and 1880s, is the result of a schism between the secular section and the very rich and powerful older establishment of Court, Society and Church, which still set the tone, gave the example and called the tune. One could draw an analogy between these two sets of values and the famous dispute between the Church of England and Darwin over the implications of the theory of evolution. There are always exceptions, and the more adventurous of the clergy, from informed and cultured backgrounds, certainly patronized the new artists and the new aesthetic.

The greatest artist in the medium of stained glass at the end of the nineteenth century was to be Burne-Jones. His close association with William Morris in the 1870s, 80s and 90s produced a wide range of windows that perhaps have only lately been appreciated for their true worth. Morris for the most part designed the surrounds and the scroll-work infills together with the borders, while Burne-Jones supplied the figures and background details in his own inimitable style of drawing. It is a mistake to think of Burne-Jones as in any way attached to the Gothic Revival movement. For one thing he arrived on the scene too late; for another his real loyalty was to the Florentine draughtsmanship of Ghirlandaio and Botticelli. Burne-Jones's power of silhouette and arabesque in figurative design has never been bettered in English art, and it was just this quality that made it possible for him to design for glass with the minimum of discomfort in his style. Although many of his windows are placed in Gothic, or even Romanesque, embrasures, the designs have a fifteenth-century Italian quality which was his especial hall-mark, though one would not call him a plagiarist. The three windows he designed for Christchurch Cathedral in Oxford, for instance, are all very different from one another, and yet each could be considered a masterpiece.

The detail of a Morris/Burne-Jones window repays attention. Morris took immense care to get the craftsmanship right. Every stroke of the brush has a delicacy and exactitude that ensures the window is of the highest quality. Burne-Jones's colour-schemes were of a new order, very much influenced by the influx of far-eastern artefacts and fabrics associated with the Aesthetic Movement. His greatest works are undoubtedly the windows he designed in the 1880s in Birmingham for the cathedral designed by William Archer. Archer was perhaps the most accomplished architect of the early eighteenth century in England after Wren and Vanburgh, and his highly original Baroque hall-church in the centre of Birmingham was an ideal setting for the three round-headed windows circling the apse and the one large rounded window at the west end under the tower. As in many baroque buildings the windows to either side of the chancel are themselves bent round a quadrant. To attempt this was a technical challenge. At the end is a traditional subject for the exit from a church. It was used in many transept schemes in French cathedrals towards the end of the Middle Ages. Here the subject is pushed to its ultimate possibility of expression; the use of reds and golden colour and dark pinks and slate greys, and the division of the tall window into three horizontal zones – with human spectators at the base, the rocking rhythm of the buildings being violently destroyed in the middle zone, and the angelic heralds swaying menacingly from side to side at the top – makes this one of the masterpieces of stained glass of the nineteenth century. The design, which owes much indeed to the inspiration from early-Renaissance sources, as can be seen in the drapery and the disposition and character of the colours, also seems to me to be aware of qualities that were quite novel to western art in the 1880s, transposed from Japanese prints. These prints were on the market for the first time, and their highly unexpected linear composition, and disturbing use of multiple diagonals for the dramatic effect seem to have been incorporated into the Burne-Jones design for the Last Judgement window at Birmingham.

The number of good artists employed in the design of stained glass in the nineteenth century in England was legion. Holman Hunt, Ford Madox Brown, both off-shoots of the Pre-Raphaelites, designed windows which had an allure of their own. The best designer after Burne-Jones in my opinion is Henry Holliday, who was even more in love with the ethos of the early-Renaissance than Burne-Jones. He was not as good a painter, as we can see in his only truly famous (or infamous) picture, that of Dante meeting Beatrice on the Lungarno at Florence. But his designs for stained glass have an astonishing integrity and serenity.

Despite having partially freed itself from the Gothic Revival yoke, during the 1870s and 80s, stained glass was still subject to the delegated art system. Every art which is pursued on a large scale is a delegated art. But delegation is difficult and calls for the utmost sensitivity when it comes to fine or decorative art. In no sphere is this more crucial than in stained glass. The solution to this dilemma in Victorian times was for the designing painter to prepare the most meticulous cartoons, full-scale, with every nuance clearly delineated. This eliminated the least possibility of the painter's designs being distorted when they were interpreted in glass.

William Morris was responsible for a further development in the art world – the quintessentially English Arts and Crafts movement. This was to bring back the personal commitment and the personal touch to every facet of the decorative arts. Although it only began in the 1890s, it subsequently gathered strength and really belongs to the history of the early twentieth century when it came fully to fruition. However, something must be said about it here since it was the expression of the urge against the march of the machine which Morris initiated.

The tenet of the Arts and Crafts movement was that every artefact in every different craft had to receive the stamp of the maker; it had, in fact, to be a 'work of art'. The two parts of William Morris's dictum quoted above – 'only tolerate in your house what you know to be useful and what you believe to be beautiful' – were fused together. This was an all but impossible brief to follow all the time in all departments of the decorative arts simultaneously, and it is not surprising that, in the main, the movement failed. Nevertheless, during the short time of its influence, it did produce astonishing results in furniture, in ceramic design (the so-called 'studio potters') and in stained glass, as well as in silverware and jewelry.

Painters who had been trained in the disciplines of drawing and painting at the newly opened regional and metropolitan art schools could, if they wished, opt for additional disciplines such as printmaking and stained glass. This helped to free the craft of glass from the supply-merchants, and a great deal of highly original and creative design between 1890 and 1930 resulted. The personality of the 'artist' in the medium came to the fore – not only as delegating-designer but as actual painter-executant as well. Hence the great vitality of stained glass towards the end of the nineteenth century and beyond.

What was left of the Gothic Revival is typified by the fabric of Liverpool Anglican Cathedral. Designed by the grandson of the original high Victorian Gothic architect Giles Gilbert Scott, this enormous edifice took some eighty years to build. Almost all the glass in the building originated from the firm of Whitefriars, and the particular stamp of its designer, John Hogan, is in every window. It must be said that on a large scale (and the cathedral is on the very

*Hollyhocks* by John LaFarge, now in the Pennsylvania Academy of Fine Arts (Audiovisual Collection of the Stained Glass Association of America)

largest scale) the effect is impressive, but when seen close to the defects of the design become apparent.

In France, when the significance of the Gothic Revival began to dawn, there was remarkable activity as a result of Prosper Merimée, the author and novelist, being made head of the Monuments of France in the 1840s. He arranged that recordings of every site of importance throughout France were made. Merimée's encouragement was behind the restoration of many secular castles and buildings of the Middle Ages after some four hundred years of neglect. In this he was indebted to the architect and antiquarian Viollet-le-Duc, the publication of whose famous *Dictionnaire Raisonnée de l'Architecture* was the *ne plus ultra* of information on things Gothic. Viollet-le-Duc undertook great projects such as the restoration of the fourteenth-century Château de Pierrefonds, an enormous pile. He also reconstituted the entire walled city of Carcassonne in the Midi. When it came to the restoration of the French cathedrals Viollet-le-Duc was indispensible. Hardly one major or minor church in France escaped his attentions in the course of his professional life. The main energy of France was towards restoration, and the deep tradition of scholarship in art, architecture, stained glass and the decorative arts that we associate with France dates from the middle of the nineteenth century. As a result of the efforts initiated by Prosper Merimée and Viollet-le-Duc the medieval glass of France is in first-rate condition. The research into the preservation of glass resulted obliquely in a certain influence on the theories of painting at the mid-century and beyond. There was a growth of stained-glass firms in France parallel to that of England. The amount of work to be done in restoration and original designs was enormous.

The small book published by Michel Eugène Chevreul called *The Principles of Harmony and Contrasts in Colour* was destined to have a decisive effect on French painting – and through that to affect the rest of the world's visual art. Chevreul was adviser to the Gobelins tapestry factories, and it was his work on analysing exactly what occurred when colours were contiguous that was the stimulant for the Impressionists. The interest in optical effects of colour-stimuli, juxtaposing pure colour, arose because in tapestry it is impossible

RIGHT
St Eustace's Episcopal
Church, Lake Placid, NY.
St Eustace and the stag by
Louis Comfort Tiffany
(Audiovisual Collection
of the Stained Glass
Association of America)

FAR RIGHT
St Andrew, Kimbolton.
Window by Louis
Comfort Tiffany (Photo
Painton Cowen)

Gloucester Cathedral.
The Annunciation; part
of a window in the Lady
Chapel by Christopher
Whall, 1898 (Photo Peter
Cormack)

to 'mix' colours; individual points of colour have perforce to be juxtaposed since the different coloured threads cannot do more than appear next to one another.

Although the theories – or rather discoveries – of Chevreul were primarily applied to and associated with painting and tapestry working, they were in fact equally valid for the art of stained glass, since it is not easy to change the colour in any one piece of glass.

Chevreul's object in the analysis of colour was to be able to produce tapestry with a full colour range but limit the number of colours employed, and he was successful so far as the Gobelins works were concerned. His influence on painting, however, was totally different. For the first time the painter was given a scientific basis for his art. The colour analysis of simultaneous contrasts, which involved putting highly differentiated colour in close proximity, was seized upon by the Impressionists, opening up the possibilities of colour in painting far beyond what had previously been envisaged.

Subsequently, after the 1880s and 90s, which witnessed the high point of Impressionist achievement, the theories of Chevreul were taken a step further by the practice of the Pointillistes, where minute divisionism of colour into a series of tiny dots of pure colour creates a picture which seems to shimmer into a unified sensation when viewed from the appropriate distance. This vision of life as an assemblage of irridescent points of pure colour pioneered by Seurat, and other artists such as Le Sidanier, was the stuff of which stained glass was made, or should have been. But in fact the Chevreul discoveries were not directly turned back to work upon the most suitable medium, because the stained-glass world was widely separated from the world of the painter. Discoveries which were a source of invention in one medium did not necessarily spill over into another, however appropriate.

However, it is interesting that stained glass did have an effect on painting, but as the result of theories of Emile Bernard, an associate of Paul Gauguin. Bernard was concerned to rediscover a valid basis for the image which he considered had been eroded away by Impressionism's concentration on appearances and effects. Bernard noticed the Impressionist approach was tending towards the complete destruction of the traditional, memorative, basis of art. Each picture in the Impressionist manner was only one frame, as it were, from the sequence of our existence, and what happened before and after that particularized instant simply did not exist. In the ideas he had towards forging an image that was of in-depth significance, with associations and values not immediately reliant on purely visual observation, Emile Bernard cited primitive art and medieval art and particularly drew attention to the art of stained glass as practised in the thirteenth and fourteenth centuries. In these instances he saw an art that had an almost metaphysical foundation – a foundation of belief, a belief that went far further and deeper than the iridescent surface-values of Impressionism.

To concentrate solely on the relationship between painting, stained glass and the various aesthetic theories going around in the 1880s and 90s is to ignore the main vehicle for glass, architecture. Here again the general record of France at the beginning of what is called *La Belle Epoque* (1871–1914) is not particularly inspiring. The achievements in the new style of architecture now known as the '*Jugendstyl*' or 'Art Nouveau' are better examined in Belgium and Holland and, what is left of it, in Vienna. Here we see the conviction of the style in full force. The factors going towards the make-up of a building must not only have relevance in themselves and towards one another but a certain over-all aesthetic philosophy must be expressed. The buildings of the Low Countries and, eccentrically, Spain, at this time show a well-informed concern for the integration of glass, tiles, stained glass, metalwork, wood and plaster; so much so that for almost the first time since the middle of the eighteenth century a style in which the decorative element was completely inseparable from the articulation of the broad masses of the building was brought into being. All were in unity giving a sense of harmony and orchestrated expression. The result was an irresistible movement of energetic twisting forms.

Although the inspiration of Art Nouveau seems to derive from observations in nature, of insect carapaces, bones, wing-structures, flower and leaf formation, and sea-animals and plants, it is allied to sound nineteenth-century engineering practice.

The results of this preoccupation with organic form and novelty of construction and expression gave life to an architectural style which found no difficulty in straddling the solidly formal and the outrageously decorative. Art Nouveau was a success while it lasted but it was destined to be abandoned in favour of a more geometric style almost before the implication of the system had worked towards a final flowering. Nevertheless there were several masterpieces of the style, one of which is the great dome over the staircase at the corner of Galleries Lafayette in Paris.

# The Twentieth Century

The real watershed between the Victorian era and our own was the 1914–18 war. The first years of the twentieth century were ones of great diversification and inventiveness for stained glass in England. But it would be a mistake to think there was any particularly coherent pattern to the activities of stained-glass artists in Europe, or in America.

Towards the latter part of the nineteenth century and at the beginning of the twentieth there were two artists of genius who specialized in stained glass working in America. John LaFarge and Louis Tiffany would have been champions in any country in which they might have been born. As it is, the period between 1880 and 1910 was one of the most astonishing from the point of view of art that America has seen. Not only were there architects of world stature, such as Louis Sullivan and Frank Lloyd Wright, but the general commercial and cultural atmosphere demanded more and more in the way of performance. Cash was no object. Consequently LaFarge and Tiffany were presented with opportunities which simply did not occur in Europe, and they took them.

Tiffany was the son of the most prestigious and richest jeweler in New York and had all the advantages anyone with imagination and drive could wish for. He seemed to have unlimited funds, initially at least, and all the opportunity to carry out his ideas with the minimum of opposition. The result was a series of technically most ingenious windows. His style depended on a richness of natural colour and form which entailed a wide range of tonal contrasts – more extreme than had hitherto been thought appropriate in the medium of glass. There was no technique of which he was not master and he invented new ones when necessary. He needed all the expertise he could acquire, because his designs involved naturalistic details of subjects that had previously not been considered feasible. Tiffany's designs included bunches of roses, wisteria hanging from a pergola, with each floret in each raceme having a precise descriptive treatment, hollyhocks and delphiniums, whole orange trees and lemon trees and many more. The spatial element was not left out either since, in the interests of verisimilitude, there had to be a background and a middleground too. As a consequence the pergolas were posed against blue landscapes of distant hills. Cloud and sunlight abounded. There was as deep an effect of illusion as could possibly be obtained in the medium – and all of this was executed in romantic, almost technicolour. Tiffany also broke new ground in the size and shape of the pieces of glass he used. Up to now, most stained-glass designers had felt it necessary to make the pieces of glass roughly the same size as one another. This was to achieve an even-rhythmed feeling over the surface area of the glass. If we contrast Tiffany with an English designer working at the same time, Edward Burne-Jones, we realize the English artist would have considered it intolerable to have taken such liberties with the lead-intervals; there is no such breath-taking freedom in his work. The convention that Burne-Jones followed was one that had been hammered out by William Morris after having studied fifteenth-century windows. It was, despite the study, a thoroughly Victorian convention. Tiffany on the other hand either did not have an inkling of this, or if he did, cared not a whit for it. His intervals in the leading are exactly suited to what he wanted to depict and express. When there were myriads of little details, made up of thousands of florets or leaves, and if there had to be a change of colour between these tiny parts in order to distinguish them, Tiffany piled on the leadwork and produced a maze of little leads closely following the natural forms of what he was depicting. Conversely, in the background and in the treatment of the more architectural details and human figures, the scale of interval between the leads expanded dramatically; the glass assumed large irregularly shaped areas. If there was a physical necessity for leadwork to be introduced that was not strictly part of the visual

St Cuthbert's, Edinburgh.
Window by Louis
Comfort Tiffany (Photo
Painton Cowen)

design, Tiffany was not above placing a straight line of lead across the composition. He calculated, quite rightly, that the eye would straddle the gap between the realism of the design and the convention of the means of execution, tending simply to ignore the intrusive line of the construction (if it was in a straight line) much as we all tend to ignore the forest of television masts nowadays when we view modern housing. As a result, Tiffany's designs, from a purely ocular and technical point of view, are highly original and effective. The motivation behind the designs, however, is considerably more complex – and, to my mind, less successful.

One cannot accuse Tiffany of outright plagiarism, since the most obvious instance in painting from which he could have borrowed had not been executed yet. I refer to the series of enormous paintings by Claude Monet, based on his gardens at Giverny, outside Paris, and called *Les Nymphaeas*. But Tiffany must have been well aware of the paintings done by the Impressionists. He might well have crossed the Atlantic to see the latest artistic successes in Paris and Vienna. The atmospheric unity of colouring in late Claude Monet paintings is most accurately echoed in the shimmering effects in glass of a large Tiffany window. The designer in glass was assuming the eye and the judgement of the painter and unifying the wide 'canvas' of the stained-glass window much as a painter unified his canvas. Tiffany was largely responsible for this new approach.

However, I have some serious reservations about Tiffany's designs. In many of the larger compositions there is the hint of the meretricious for all their astonishing technical command. A miasma of the pretty, the appealing, the picture postcard even, and the sentimentality of the valentine and the Christmas greeting hangs over many of Tiffany's ideas. It is as if a potential vulgarity, held in check most of the time, only needed the slightest stimulus to break out.

In contrast, LaFarge, as a stained-glass innovator of genius, has only quite recently begun to be acknowledged. His simple effort to portray flowers and objects in glass resulted in the minting of a visual language that was entirely original. The invention of the irregular line, the plastic and expressive line, in the leadwork of LaFarge's

*Spring* by John LaFarge, formerly in Whitney Residence, New York, now in the Philadelphia Museum of Art (Audiovisual Collection of the Stained Glass Association of America)

Winchelsea Parish
Church, Sussex. Detail of
east window, Christ in
Majesty, by Douglas
Strachan, 1929. (Photo
Peter Cormack)

panels enabled him to expand his range far wider than any artist working in the medium at that time.

The innovation of LaFarge's compositions has something in common with the transformation of Dutch flower painting in the seventeenth century. In Holland the seventeenth century began with tight little bunches of flowers, each painstakingly painted, every flower demurely in place with the same hard all-over focus on every part of the composition. By the end of the century the Dutch had evolved a quite new aesthetic regarding flower painting. They found they could move the elements of the composition around, creating a world of more rhythmic vitality, subtlety and sensitive response to the various phenomena we see around us. Something of this sort was behind LaFarge's transformation of the hitherto static, staid and perhaps stodgy world of the stained-glass panel.

LaFarge's placement of colour is unexpected and successful. The relationship between the border (always to be freely interpreted and treated) and the background and the subject shows an awareness and a sophistication that was new to the medium. And it was, as was Tiffany's work, triumphantly of our own time.

Yet the methods LaFarge used were relatively simple and direct. There is aciding but it does not dominate to the same degree as it does with Tiffany. In this LaFarge is closer to the Europeans in that he does not rely on technical novelty to underpin his valid formal position. He never employs technicalities for their own sake. As a result his work is fresh and open in a way that Tiffany's is not. In LaFarge's panels the different parts move in relation to one another in a new and lissom way. The hitherto stiff and clumsy medium glass (if we compare it to the delicate and mercurial possibilities of painting, for instance) is made to dance in the most delightful way. I think that LaFarge was quite as aware as Tiffany of the developments in painting on the other side of the Atlantic, but he was also aware, surely, of the extraordinary sense of placing and interval displayed in Japanese painting and printmaking. At about that time these artefacts from Japan were being imported for the first time in large quantities.

JOSEPH OF ARIMATHEA AN HONOVRABLE

COVNSELLOR WHICH ALSO WAITED FOR THE KINGDOM OF GOD

TO THE GLORY OF GOD AND IN THANKFVLNESS FOR THE LIFE OF MAJOR SIR GRAN— VILLE CHARLES HASTINGS WHELER BART. C.B.E. J.P. D.L. M.P. B. OCT. 2. 1872. D. DEC. 14. 1927.

LaFarge's output was tantalisingly limited. He did not have a factory system as Tiffany seems to have had. As a consequence every piece has an authenticity and gives the impression of personal caring that is almost unknown in the history of stained glass. His art is the nearest that stained glass ever approached to the experience of the 'easel picture'. I do not mean to suggest by this that LaFarge tried to give the autonomous panel of stained glass a spurious quality of transparent painting – eliminating all leads, for instance, and using transparent enamels which could be fused together. The astonishing thing about him is that he managed to transform the possibilities of stained glass whilst remaining true to the classic means of expression – i.e. pieces of different coloured glass, painted, and joined together with lead.

While America was in the forefront of innovation in the medium of stained glass, there was a great push towards new expression in England and Scotland. The influence of the continental Art Nouveau or *Jugendstyl* was more apparent in the work of Glasgow-based Charles Rennie Mackintosh than in London or England as a whole. Mackintosh was an architect of genius, a highly original talent which extended to the designing of every detail of the buildings in which he was involved. In some cases this included stained glass, and Mackintosh's contribution to the medium, although normally on an exceedingly small scale, was important for its originality. He used no paint to qualify the glass – created no images beyond that of the leadwork – but, for the first time utilized the opal and opalescent glasses that were available for stained-glass work. His vision was noted all over the continent, especially in pre-1914 Germany. Mackintosh was employed in many small commercial ventures such as tea-shops, which inevitably had a fashionable but short existence and much has by now been destroyed. Enough remains, however, to demonstrate what an original talent he had.

The clean and simple tonality of Mackintosh's version of Art Nouveau, with its control of spatial emphasis, and consequent subtle manipulation of volume, involving the exact calculation of light and the way it falls in the interior of rooms and entrances, was something quite special to him.

All Saints, Slough. Alfred Wolmark, early 20C

The other stained-glass artist of note to come from Scotland at that time was Douglas Strachan. He was a stained-glass artist, not an architect, and was heavily influenced by both the Art Nouveau and by the later paintings of Sir Edward Burne-Jones, particularly the *Perseus* series. Strachan's art was very similar to that of Tiffany in that he pushed every means available on the technical side to give his art an over-all mysteriously romantic quality. The interior atmosphere generated by Strachan's windows is inevitably subdued and dim. It is as though Strachan had taken the *Perseus* series, with its odd, other-world colouring, sinuous arabesques and slippery rhythms and attempted to build a whole aesthetic on it. He was only partly successful in the final result. In the Scottish War Memorial, built in Edinburgh Castle after the 1914–18 war by Sir Robert Lorimer, Strachan's glass produces an unreal atmosphere that in the end becomes almost repellent. The mazy lushness of the windows produces a feeling of claustrophobia.

Strachan's oeuvre is enormous, since his art exactly fitted everybody's expectations of what the medium could, and should, do. The best place to see it, in my opinion, is the strangely beautiful medieval church at Winchelsea in Sussex, England. St Thomas's choir is all that remains of a far larger church. The whole range of windows was filled at intervals by Strachan, financed by Lord Forteviot, the whisky billionaire. As a consequence there is not the unity one might otherwise have expected. Though nothing is in bad taste it is evident that Strachan's capabilities in colour, whatever his formidable capabilities in the art of painting on glass were, never rose above the obvious and the commonplace. None the less the church, taken as a whole, is an amazing achievement, having an almost Arthur Rackham atmosphere about it.

There were many original and talented artists in Britain at the turn of the century who were working more or less along Art Nouveau lines. Chief among them was Christopher Whall, whose delightful, whimsical and, at times, very tart little book of instruction on the art of stained glass is still the best of its sort in existence. Whall was the outstanding practitioner of his day and his distinctive style was employed widely enough. The glazing of the lady chapel of Gloucester Cathedral is probably the greatest monument to his art. The design is very much better than that of Strachan, though still roughly in the same idiom. Christopher Whall's technique of painting, though not as astonishingly accomplished as that of Douglas Strachan, is attractive and subtle. His control of textures – meaningful textures – is marvellously evocative in the way it delicately manipulates the flow of light coming into the building, creating a comfortable and pleasant atmosphere. Whall inserted a large window in the north transept of Canterbury Cathedral that is well worth seeing. Fortunately it survived the 1939–45 war despite having been left in situ. The delineation of character and the finesse of the detailing brings to mind not so much a painter as a sculptor, in fact the sculptor Alfred Gilbert. Gilbert was the inspiration for achievement in many arts other than his own, Christopher Whall's for one.

Of the numerous lesser artists of the period, two particularly deserve mention. Karl Parsons is not well known but he produced some good work. It has a clean cut, almost woodcut, quality and his drawing was, in common with much at that time, superbly economical and efficient. I have particular affection for his art since he was the teacher of my master E. J. Nuttgens. They both, at various times, taught at the Royal College of Art, London.

There were two outstanding nonagenarian architects of immensely differing talents and interest. Everyone has heard of the American architect Frank Lloyd Wright; he lived for so many years one wondered whether he would ever die. His early houses are filled with examples of his stained glass.

Wright's designs rarely condescend into the curvature of a line except in the case of the Guggenheim Museum in New York where there is hardly a straight one. This preference for straight lines and uncompromising plane-changes did not detract from his amazing mastery of the diagonal line. The diagonal is notoriously difficult to employ successfully in architecture since its restless energy and consequent tearaway effect can be very destructive. Wright's ability to balance diagonal against diagonal is best seen in the Philadelphia Synagogue but it also contributed a unique quality to his designs of

Robie House, Chicago.
Dining room windows by
Frank Lloyd Wright, 1909
(Photo G. Smythe,
Architectural Association
Slide Library)

stained glass. The sense of interval in Wright's glass, together with his elegant leading (never heavy) and the motifs he used (usually Modern or inspired by art of the North American Indian Navajo tribe) assure him a permanent niche in the annals of glass. It is still possible to learn much from Frank Lloyd Wright.

The other nonagenarian was the Englishman, Sir Ninian Comper. Comper used a hopelessly outmoded Gothic-Renaissance-Baroque idiom – something peculiar to himself which he referred to as 'Unity by *In*clusion' – and remained firmly outside the whole Modern Movement of which he was just as scornful as they were about him. As a result Comper has been unjustly neglected as an artist and as a stained-glass designer. In fact, within his own self-imposed limits, to which he strictly adhered, Comper was a subtle and noteworthy colourist. His best work was in areas over which others took no pains. The *traceries* of the windows Comper designed, in the very late Gothic style are set out and calculated very much as moves in chess or at bridge or poker are made. Everything is worked out to a nicety and this passes the casual viewer by. He would have no notion that he was looking at the work of one of the cleverest manipulators of colour-stimuli in the business.

At the turn of the century the Irish Renaissance in letters was in full swing. Lady Gregory, A. E., George Bernard Shaw, J. M. Synge, and above all W. B. Yeats, ensured that the whole world was aware of the significance of Irish writers.

Where letters had pioneered art was not long to follow. The painters of the period, such as Jack Yeats (W. B.'s brother) and Sir William Orpen, were matched by three stained-glass designers of great talent. They were associated with the 'Tower of Glass' in Dublin which was set up as a centre and workshop for stained glass at the turn of the century. Harry Clarke was perhaps the most famous; certainly he was the most outstanding from a technical point of view and his powers of drawing and composition were of the highest order. His idiom was mysterious and deeply romantic, even at times morbid. The gaunt, phthisical heads and hands protrude out of the most impossibly swinging and clinging drapery; the colour one can only describe as 'Celtic'. The whole has a hot-house, gloxinia-like intensity, a quality of uneasy opulence and decadence; yet it is great art much in the same way that Aubrey Beardsley's art can be called great. The drawing and placement, and above all the feelings running through the glass, seem very much in the idiom of Beardsley of whom Clarke, apparently, denied all knowledge.

The two other great artists connected to the activities of the Tower of Glass were Michael Healy and, for a short time, Wilhelmina Geddes. Healy is an almost totally neglected artist. His interest was solely in stained glass and his work may be seen in the provinces of the Republic of Ireland, principally in Roscrea Cathedral on the extreme west coast. Those who take the trouble to go and see the work of Healy (and of Clarke) in this cathedral will be astonished by its extraordinary quality. There seems to be in Healy's designs a definite attempt to emulate, if not surpass, the intricacy and elaboration of the Book of Kells. All the glass has been subjected to the most painstaking and minutely detailed aciding technique, layer of glass over layer. This results in the most extraordinary shimmering pointilliste effects. Luckily Healy's sense of colour was fully up to the demands of the medium and he produced a series of highly individual windows.

Wilhelmina Geddes's style owes something to that of Charles

Ricketts, who was a friend of hers. The greatest of her commissions was the rose window in the newly rebuilt St Martin's Cathedral at Ypres, Flanders. Elsewhere her designs always excited controversy for their vehemence and scarcely-suppressed aggression. Yet the colour was superb, the best of the early twentieth century, and her design and execution of painting on glass has not been bettered. She was accorded a singular back-handed compliment when her window above the altar in Laleham Church, Staines, Middlesex, was removed, on the petition of the parishioners, to the back of the church (where it still is to be seen) on the grounds that it reminded them of Hell.

English glass at the turn of the century was more or less within the older tradition, a style in which the Gothic of the Revival period was tempered by an admixture of Art Nouveau. There was no modernity, as we know the term today. The reason for this is that the clergy of the Church of England at that time ensured that all expressive art commissioned under their aegis was what 'ordinary folks' could readily understand and therefore radical innovation in stained glass was extremely rare.

However, there is one shining example of real originality from this period, the three-light window at the west end of All Saints, Slough. This window was the first fully non-figurative design as such to be executed in England. It dates from around the World War I era, and apparently was the sole stained-glass commission of the Vorticist painter and friend of Wyndham Lewis, Alfred Wolmark. The window is of stunning quality, enhanced by the circumstances of its placement. All Saints is a rather conventional late Gothic Revival church in brick and stone with no special quality in its design. All the glass as you enter is very easy on the eye and reassuring in a soothing sort of way, typical of the F.S. Eden and William Kempe tradition. When one turns round, after three-quarters of an hour attending the service, the window by Wolmark at the end of the church instantly dispels any feelings of cosy illusion one might have built up. All is blasted away by the passionate intensity of the unpainted colour in the window. As Wolmark only seemingly produced this one example, stained glass lost a practitioner who could have been a landmark in English art. As it is the trail he blazed in solitude was ignored for some forty years in England – until the nave windows in Coventry Cathedral saw the light of day.

After the Art Nouveau period the art of stained glass in England once again lost contact with the world of painting. By the 1920s stained glass had become the enclave of a tight little clique who pandered to the establishment – always sure of a job by timidly toeing the line. There are exceptions but on the whole it is accurate, which is why the inter-war years seem now to have been so dull.

E. J. Nuttgens, whom I mentioned earlier as a pupil of Karl Parsons, was one of the exceptions. The major part of his commissions came from the Catholic Church in England and consequently he was relieved of the necessity of conforming with the established ideas of stained glass as applied to the Church of England. His colour is fresh and clear and his powers of draughtsmanship were second to none. He was the best painter on glass of his own and subsequent generations, and he died at the age of ninety-two with his powers almost totally undiminished.

What was happening in the rest of Europe in the first half of the century? There was a very thin tradition in France, if we compare it with Great Britain. This was because the tight bonds that existed between church and state had been totally destroyed and dissolved by the Secularization of 1905 in France. The Catholic Church was deprived of all its buildings, its hospitals, schools, investments and property in general as a result of a furiously anti-clerical clique coming into political power. The cathedrals were confiscated along with the episcopal palaces and the whole ecclesiastical patrimony was put under the aegis of the Ministère des Beaux Arts.

World War I, with its ghastly casualties, seemed to have healed the rift between the clerical and the anti-clerical factions in France. The church had an opportunity to renew itself in relationship with much that was of great value in the world of the modern painter in France. There was a new openness towards the adoption of constructive and original ideas in architecture with the older traditions having been swept clean away.

Two examples, among many, suffice to demonstrate this. The first

Romsey Abbey, Hampshire. St Margaret by Charles E. Kempe, late 19C (Photo Painton Cowen)

OVERLEAF LEFT
St Maximim, Metz. Windows designed by Jean Cocteau, late 20C (Photo Painton Cowen)

OVERLEAF RIGHT
Ste Clothilde, Paris. Window designed and made by François-Emile Décorchement in *pâte de verre*. Art Deco, 1920s

is the Church of Ste Clothilde. This was built in the Art Deco style as a memorial to the dead of the 1914–18 war. It has survived not only physically, even with the construction of the *périférique* some fifty yards away, but also the change in taste. All the glass is by the celebrated decorative glass designer François-Emile Décorchement. He is chiefly remembered in collecting circles today for his employment of *Pâte de Verre,* his own invention. This was a technique of reducing coloured glass to tiny sherds, carefully rearranging the coloured 'sand' and 'gravel' produced, and then re-fusing all together. Décorchement's glass vessels now sell for huge sums of money. Three immense windows dominate the nave of the church on the right hand side as you enter. The general effect is stunning and, so far as I know, his work is unique. The colour is very much of the Art Deco period. Violent blues, deeply toned, make up the tops of the giant lunettes and this blue is in consonance with the intense pinks, yellows and apple greens which bring to mind the paintings by Sophie Tauber-Arp, and Sonia and Roger Delaunay. The windows around the altar are of less striking originality. Their use of the same intense blue shot through with an uncompromising scarlet recalls the decorations of the Folies Bergères. Once again the French have produced something inimitable and sensational.

The second example from the inter-war years in France is the church of Notre Dame du Raincy outside the Porte des Lilacs, on the outskirts of Paris. Again we are on the tracks of a once-celebrated but now unjustly neglected masterpiece. This is a co-operation between the architect Auguste Perret and the painter Maurice Denis (a founder-member of the painting group '*les Nabis*') together with the designer in stained glass, Marguerite Huré. The church was rather cheaply constructed and the carcass of reinforced-concrete pierced panels, of which it is made, is in a parlous condition. This does not detract from the magnificence inside. As you enter the church you are immediately aware that you are in the presence of originality. The extraordinary quality of the light that steals into the interior, investing it with an even glow of the greatest gentleness, in spite of the very strong colour employed, is reminiscent of the atmosphere in the Sainte Chapelle. But it is not so oppressive.

154

ORA PRO ANIMABUS GILBERTI K CHESTERTON (OBIIT 1936
ET FRANCISCAE CONSORTIS (OBIIT 1938)

Beaconsfield Roman
Catholic Church,
Buckinghamshire. St
Francis of Assisi window
by J. E. Nuttgens, 1938
(Photo Peter Cormack)

RIGHT
St John the Divine, New
York. Detail of window
by Charles Connick, early
20C (Photo Painton
Cowen)

BROADCASTING

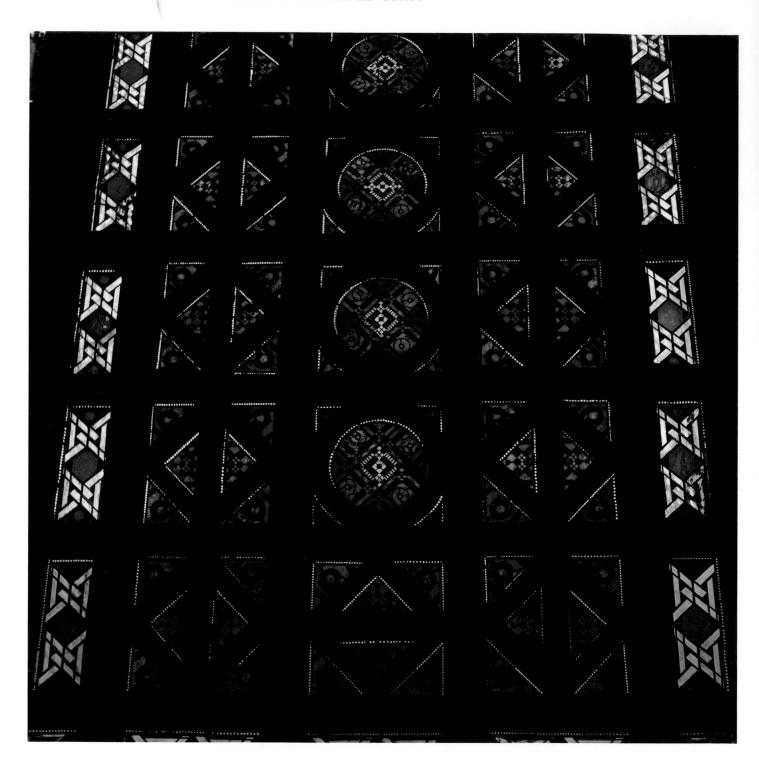

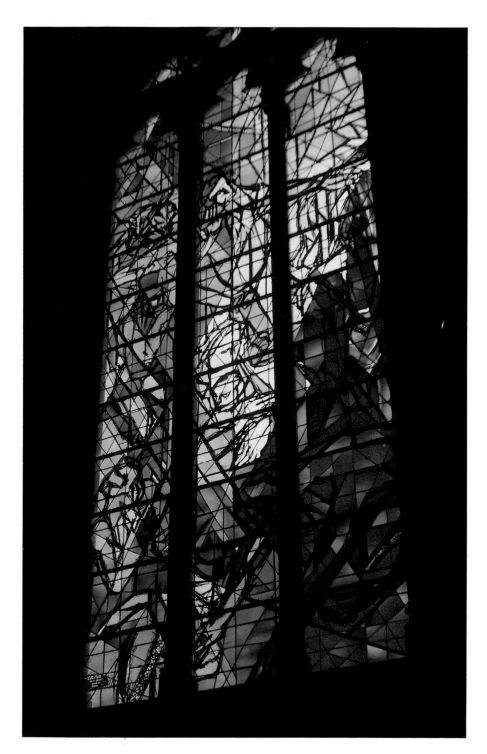

OPPOSITE
Notre Dame du Raincy,
Paris. Window by
Marguerite Huré,
designer of non-figurative
glass in *béton armé* panels
devised by Auguste
Perret, 1920s

LEFT
Metz Cathedral, Chapelle
du Saint Sacrement.
Detail of a range of
windows by Jacques
Villon, mid 20C

All Saints, Tudely, Kent. Drowning girl, detail of Crucifixion, by Marc Chagall, mid 20c (Photo Painton Cowen)

RIGHT
Varengeville-sur-Mer, Normandy. Rose window by Georges Braque at back of church, 1950s

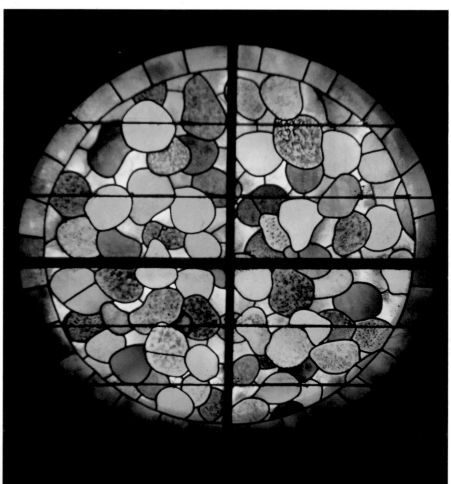

The bays of Notre Dame du Raincy are distinguished by being characterized by colour. Each bay, two by two of opposite, corresponding, windows, is coloured basically blue, or green or purple or red. The general 'set' of the colour owes nothing to anything previously employed in stained glass. The colours are 'flower-derived'; the yellows are of helianthus and marigold, the blues are of cineraria or delphinium, the red is *Lychnis chalcedonicum* and the pink, fuchsia or cyclamen. Set high up in each bay are large panels of figurative glass designed by Maurice Denis, John Piper, the English artist, has described these as 'a concession to the clergy' but I think they are something more serious than that, for they are effective in preventing the tiny windowlets of Marguerite Huré's abstract designs from massing together and producing an uncomfortable buzzing on the eye. The blander and more expansive design of the figurative panels may indeed look dated and gawky (Maurice Denis after all had never designed stained glass before) but artistically they are necessary for the general well-being of the whole. It was a risk to set two such different styles together but they are reconciled by the over-all colour harmony.

The colossal despondency and uncertainty of the inter-war period in Germany was exacerbated by hyper-inflation and the rise of the Nazis. By 1933, when the Nazis were fully established, there was not a great deal of activity on the part of the churches, either Catholic or Protestant. From the point of view of building or re-building churches the inter-war years in Germany were rather disappointing. Over the border in Holland, however, the situation was much more encouraging. There was no such thing as a built-in market for ecclesiastical goods in Holland as the ecclesiastical lobby was relatively unimportant and weak. This meant that the medium of stained glass was free to explore new relationships with the visions of painters – the pioneering non-figurative painters of the 20s and 30s. The stained-glass panel *per se* came back into the public's consciousness.

Between the wars America to some extent seemed to be in limbo so far as the modern styles in stained glass were concerned. After the Wall Street crash of 1929, which spelt the sudden demise of the

Art Deco style, the brighter echelons of the architectural world eagerly received the theories and practices arising out of the activities of the Bauhaus movement in inter-war Germany. Since the theoretical basis of the Bauhaus was severely reductive – rendering everything into a 'rational' cone, cylinder, pyramid and cube – there seemed no place at all for the art of stained glass. It was categorized generally as an unnecessary and sentimental excrescence. Another contributory factor was the inability to recognize the importance of the *interplay* factor that takes place between form and light in all good architecture. Form became the be-all and end-all, and planes were encouraged to meet with candour and uncomplicated cleanness. Now whenever planes meet unequivocally in architecture, and especially if this is accompanied by an almost sacred respect for *construction,* the sensitivity to the flow of light in and around architecture is very largely lost. If an architect is fundamentally insensitive to what light can do to the interior of a building there is no role assigned to stained glass. The call for the medium dwindles to nil. This was the overall situation so far as major building projects were concerned from 1935 to 1975 in the United States. No architect made use of glass for a major project except possibly Marcel Breuer at a Benedictine monastery. There, he employed the colour-theorist Joseph Albers for a truly original window in the baptistry.

The smaller project was another matter. America is, after all, a vast country with plenty of niches where people can set up workshops and realize their own individual convictions. Ultimately it was in precisely these quarters that the new possibilities of working in coloured, though mostly not painted, glass started reasserting themselves. But it started in a small way and did not make much impression until well into the 60s.

There is a similarity in the architectural scenes of both the United States and Great Britain between the years 1929 and 1975. These were the years which witnessed an unbridgeable chasm between the Modern Movement on the one hand and the more traditional styles (largely attached by this time to church-building alone) which had an historical basis. There was plenty of life in the historical styles – for certain purposes. Gothic was still heavily employed for church building of all denominations. At Yale University it was even used, in the shape of a perpendicular-styled tower, as an ingenious disguise to house five gymnasiums, one on top of the other. The National Gallery of America in Washington D.C. was boldly designed in very high-class Classical style almost at the same time as the Empire State building was being finished in New York.

The great Gothic glass designer Charles Connick, of Boston, Mass., stands out as a man of prodigious talent. There was no equivalent to Connick on the European scene while he was alive. George Bodley was by this time (1920s) dead, and his designs for Washington Cathedral were being carried on by others. The nineteenth century had not ceased to exist so far as Connick was concerned. His designs were impeccably crafted and within their terms of reference were almost unassailable. They were the fine flowering of a movement that had persisted for well over a century. But Connick, despite his ability, remained curiously isolated. His case reminds me of the sixteenth-century Juan Gil de Hontañon completing Gothic cathedrals at Segovia and Salamanca in Spain a hundred years after the style had collapsed in the rest of Europe.

The greatest, but by no means the only, architect who employed the Art Nouveau idiom with brilliant and shocking panache, at the same time as incorporating so much of his own invention and borrowings as to forge a completely original style, was the Spaniard Antonio Gaudí. Gaudí designed everything to do with his buildings from tiles, to ironwork, plaster, stone, concrete and timber, and when he felt it was a necessary accompaniment to his buildings he designed stained glass. Gaudí's masterpiece, La Sagrada Familia, has no glass of note in it. This is a great disappointment. The designs would have been spectacular in their originality, judging from the architecture. We can see something of what the combined effect of the interior fittings and the light from stained glass would have been by examining the general effect of the interior of Palma de Mallorca Cathedral, which was reordered by Gaudí late in the nineteenth century. Though the actual quality of the stained glass (*not* designed by Gaudí) is not good, the interplay between glass and architecture is unique and quite spectacular.

The small chapel of the Colonia Guëll, just outside Barcelona, Spain, is the sole realization of Gaudí's own design in stained glass. The technical skill involved in the windows is almost nil. The glass is not secured by lead at all, but the pieces are large enough in themselves to fit into ironwork frames – roughly the shape of daisies. The resultant windows are irregular roundels with wavy edges. They are different shapes and sizes but combine together in unison with the architecture. The colour-change in each window differs. The large pieces of glass change colour halfway down their axis – from red to blue from pink to green and so on. I suspect that Gaudí simply made use of transparent varnishes on plate or rolled glass. So much for technique, but the expressive originality of this glass is second to none.

The character of much Swiss and German inter-war stained glass was more than tinged with the Bauhaus ethic and aesthetic. There is not much left of this period to see in Germany but the glass at St Anthony's Church at Basel is typical of the new approach of 'modernism'. Figuration is mixed up with large areas of sheer colour, some of it passing muster, some of it embarrassingly inferior. The overall look of the interior is not at all bad, however. Sheets of different colours drench the bays of the church, giving some expression and liveliness to the otherwise rather austere reinforced concrete piers.

Catastrophes such as the 1939–45 war (initially in Europe and eventually all over the world) enable history to be defined very clearly. Everything before the war was of one ethos or tenor and everything after was of quite another. This was no less true of stained glass than of any other art-form.

The material damage to the fabric of Europe is, at the end of the century, difficult for those not witnesses to comprehend. The achievement of stained glass artists and designers after the war was an outcome of the destruction, since so much had either to be restored or replaced altogether. The act of replacement was not merely a practical matter. It was far more an act of spiritual regrowth and re-appraisal, and this attitude had a profound effect on the aesthetic ideas of the time. But these ideas were not parallel in every

European country, and the resultant nationally based aesthetics differ very widely in their emphasis and expression. Stained glass being an art that depends, like theatre, on a consensus vote of the general public, was also influenced by public opinion. It is quite impossible to change a nation's basic assumptions as to what is beautiful, expressive, attractive and of quality. This is why ideas in decorative art tend to be parochial. They are not accepted in other countries until they have become established at home and have acquired a certain stamp of connoisseur's recognition which could be called 'historicity'. Therefore it is no surprise to find little interblending of cultures and aesthetics in European stained glass after the war.

France sustained a great deal of material damage. Whole towns were swept away, some of them of inestimable historical worth, such as Rouen, Strasbourg, Caen, and Evreux. But along with the conviction that these would be rebuilt, replaced, there was a search for new expression in the arts as part of a far greater task, the psychological resuscitation of the spirit of France. Aesthetic considerations have always been of prime importance, both as status symbols and, more deeply, as witness to the healing of spiritual wounds and the reassertion of France's cultural plenitude. The fact that the state intervened quite without modesty in order to bring benefit to everyone in France is not important.

State subvention and support was evenly distributed in France after the war, on one hand, the new enterprises such as the complete rebuilding of le Havre as a sea-port, and on the other the re-investment of older edifices such as the French cathedrals with startlingly new works of art. There is no doubt that nothing would have been successfully achieved without state intervention.

Much of rebuilding of France involved religious buildings and therefore the possibilities of stained-glass commissions were great. These, in the newest churches, are not on the whole a success. Of course there are exceptions, but in the main the newest buildings of France, between 1945 and 1965 say, did not produce anything that could be seriously considered as art. Everything was too hastily chosen, too superficial in quality, had an exhibition-like impermanence about it that was basically insufficient. Great exceptions did arise, however. Chief among these is the church of St Joseph in le Havre, by Auguste Perret, who in fact was assigned the rebuilding of the whole town which he laid out very successfully in a regular pattern. This giant commission may well have been his last job. He commissioned Marguerite Huré to furnish the tower-church with stained glass on all four sides. The tower, which constitutes the body of the church, is completely hollow, capable of being lit from the inside, and thus becomes a sentinel and a beacon for the whole of le Havre and beyond. It stands some two hundred and fifty feet high. Marguerite Huré finished her life's work with the designs of this church. The disposition of the colours is masterly and their selection, which is not limited to the primaries or the spectrum, is equally authoritative. A great deal of brown, yellow and light green, together with blue make up this glorious monument to modernism and the resurgent French spirit.

The other aspect of French post-1945 interest in stained glass is of more importance to this book, namely the employment of French painters to design stained glass to be placed in the restored and reopened cathedrals and churches of France. There were many painters of great talent, some, such as Matisse and Picasso, of genius, who had not hitherto been persuaded to design for glass. The Ministère des Beaux Arts, who together with the Ministère des Bâtiments Anciens had custodianship of the greater churches of the nation, including all the cathedrals, hit on the bright idea of commissioning directly the greatest painters of the time in France to design for stained glass. Picasso declined but those who were willing were assigned various cathedrals. The cathedral of Metz alone was the recipient of windows by Jacques Villon (the Chapel of the Blessed Sacrament), Marc Chagall and Julius Bissière. Others were to follow. The greatest of the pre-war designers of stained glass such as Paul Bony and Jean Barillet undertook the refurnishing with ravishing windows of the greater cathedrals of Notre Dame de Paris, Amiens and Beauvais. Elsewhere there were windows by Georges Braque, Raoul Ubac, Georges Rouault and Alfred Manessier. The greatest success in the medium was the employment of Léger in the windows at Audincourt. This commission was suggested by the self-effacing

Metz Cathedral, Chapelle du Saint Sacrament. Detail of a range of windows by Jacques Villon, mid 20C

Musée Fernand Léger,
Biot. Autonomous panel
(Photo Painton Cowen)

OVERLEAF LEFT
Assy, Haute-Savoie. One
of a series of six small
windows by Georges
Rouault, 1950s (Photo
Painton Cowen)

OVERLEAF RIGHT
Eton College Chapel. The
Light under a Bushel,
right-hand side of
window in chancel by
John Piper, 1962,
interpreted by Patrick
Reyntiens

but highly influential Dominican Père Couturier whose friendships
with most artists in the Ecole de Paris enabled the Church in France
to reap so many benefits during the 1940s and 50s. The Audincourt
windows, in a working-class district, are an indication that the
restricted palette that Léger used was an asset when it came to
designing stained glass. They are among the very best that the
twentieth century has seen. Off the church at Audincourt there is a
baptistry by Jean-René Bazaine which again is beautiful, though
lacking the authority of the Léger windows.

Léger went on to design many panels of stained glass, most of
which are now at the great Léger Museum at Biot, Var, France.
Some of these are almost too big but the smaller square ones are
among the best examples of Léger's art. The last windows Léger
designed, at Courfaivre in the Swiss Jura, are of interest in that
they are simpler and more serene, almost resigned, than the fiery
harmonies of his first attempts in Audincourt.

Not far from the Léger windows at Courfaivre is a little-known
church at les Brézeux, in the French Jura, where the entire church
has been glazed to the designs of Alfred Manessier. The windows
take the form of fountains in small never-to-coalesce colour blobs
of the greatest delicacy. Manessier designed many windows in the
50s and 60s all over France, but perhaps the most impressive are
those at Hem-Poupon, near Lille. The use, as in Léger's case, of the
concrete-set glass known as *dalle-de-verre* is here brought to its
highest pitch of design potential. The thick glass slabs are difficult
to design well since their very simplicity is a snare for those who
cannot design with certainty and economy. I have seen few, apart
from those of Manessier and Léger, which succeed.

Some of the best windows by Rouault can be seen in a small
church high up in the Alps at Assy. They involve a lot of ingenuity
in the way of stretching the possibilities of the classic medium of
leaded glass to catch the exact nuances the painter demands. This
difficult task is the work of Paul Bony. Curiously enough the dark
lines so typical of Rouault's designs were originally inspired by
stained glass, possibly the result of his studying the theories of image-
building that Emile Bernard had formulated.

Georges Braque never directly designed glass except at the very end of his life, when he settled down at a studio in Varangeville in Normandy, France. Here in a small church in the centre of the village, he designed, and, I suspect, actually had a hand in painting, the windows. A large rose window at the west end of the church is particularly fine in its rich yet totally restrained colouring and patterning. At the end of the village there is an eleventh-century parish church which contains, in my opinion, the best stained glass of the twentieth century. This is a small window less than six feet tall which depicts, in the form of an abstract tree, the root of Jesse. It is quite impossible to describe adequately the extraordinary subtlety and harmony of the soft and delicate colouring which ranges from muted browns and beige to cerulean blue and sky blue together with aquamarine green. The light steals in by means of an undulating series of qualifications by paint – leaving the vital areas of glass unencumbered and serene. The eye hops from area to area and it is in the rhythm of the 'hop-intervals', as well as in the ravishing colour, that we experience the very deepest artistic satisfaction. The interpreter was again Paul Bony, who also interpreted the Matisse windows mentioned below. The world owes him a great debt in helping Georges Braque to accomplish what he did.

Towards the end of his life Henri Matisse was sent to convalesce after an operation to the Dominican Sisters at Vence, who had a small nursing home. In the course of his stay there the possibility arose of the chapel being rebuilt. One of the nuns came to M. Matisse with designs she had been ordered to do for stained glass. Would he please criticise them? He did just that, and the result was that he took over the entire design of the chapel himself. The architect was Maurice Novarina, who had previously designed the small church at Assy. It is not of much interest but it is adequate as a vehicle for the astonishing windows that Matisse proceeded to design. Seemingly of the utmost simplicity, the Matisse windows at Vence almost defy analysis. The two behind the altar are in the shape of indoor plants, the cactus-like shapes in green playing and swaying across a deep blue space behind. This patterning of green on blue is itself suspended in front of a ground of the most vivid yellow conceivable. It is as if

Robinson College, Cambridge. The Journey of the Magi, small window in the winter chapel by John Piper, interpreted by Patrick Reyntiens, 1980s the essence of mimosa, morning glory and aloe had come together in an unimaginable combination. The art of interval, on which the whole of Matisse's art depends, had never been employed to greater effect. For it was the exact interval between the parts, the emphases, that brought the work to its simple perfection. A price had to be paid, however. Matisse rejected the first ten greens he was given as samples for his windows thus encumbering the glass factory with tens of thousands of pounds' worth of green, and this embarrassment took the factory some seven years to work off through sales.

The windows in the so-called main body of the chapel at Vence are of even more drastically simplified form than those behind the altar. Large tulip-forms of alternate yellow and green ascend the windows in large bland areas that had not been seen since Gaudí designed his glass for the Colonia Guëll Chapel windows at Barcelona. These very large pieces of glass envisaged by Matisse were once again extremely carefully calculated as to their rhythm and effect. The tonality of the pure colours had been refined to a degree only Matisse could achieve, but there was one refinement that was the work of Paul Bony, the interpreter, and that was something that Matisse for all his genius could not have foreseen. For if you look closely at the surface of the range of main windows you will see that the blue and the green are transparent and allow the eye to go right through them so as to contact the outside world. It is almost like taking a refreshing plunge right into the middle of a swimming-pool. The yellow is another entity altogether, since this is only translucent, not transparent. It has been white-acided on the inside so as to support a delicately-textured knap, rather like a shammy-leather kid glove. The act of painting on the glass to achieve this would have been too violent and insensitive a qualification of the yellow; this explains the use of aciding instead of paint. It is in the push-pull effect of the total penetrability of the green and the blue as balanced against the prohibition on penetrability over the area of the acided yellow (which delicately inhibits and restrains the eye's expectation) that the real subtlety of Matisse's windows comes to be appreciated. But this additional quality, this vital invention, was the work of Bony, not of Matisse.

Chapelle du Rosaire, Vence. Main hall window, one of two by Henri Matisse

Very late in life Marc Chagall was introduced to the art of stained glass. One must admit that he forthwith made full use of designing for this medium. As Chagall lived to the age of ninety-nine and was working hard right up to the very end, it is no wonder that he managed to accomplish an immense amount of work in the years left to him. There is a Chagall window in most of the greater churches in France that could support one. The state paid more often than not. At Maintz Cathedral there is a range which cuts clean across the German sensibility in its indisciplined and painterly freedom from restraint. When these windows were first installed the German stained-glass fraternity were in consternation. In America there is glass by Chagall, and also by Matisse, in the Union Church of Pocantico Hills, North Tarrytown, New York.

It is unfair to say that when you have seen one Marc Chagall window you have seen the lot, but there is a certain similarity between his various attempts from first to last. But then Chagall as a painter was remarkably fixed in his general style, at least since the 1930s, and so it is not at all surprising that he should be consistent in his approach to glass. The thing that comes over is that he seems not to have learnt anything new, anything that would have modified his art, his painting, from the contact with another medium.

It is not possible to comment on everything in glass that Chagall designed. I propose to say something about a series of windows that I have never seen. The general principles of design are possible to comment on from reproduction, but the quality of the work is another matter. This cannot even be inferred from reproduction.

The small synagogue at the Hadasseh University in Jerusalem had the great good fortune to receive the gift of windows by Marc Chagall, which were inserted in its twelve windows making up a square lantern over the main area of the interior. It is fortunate that there were twelve for it enabled Chagall to choose the Twelve Tribes of Israel as a master-theme. Whether the whole building was not a great deal too small for the pressure and power coming from the stained glass it received is open to debate.

The first formal quality that is noticeable is that each window has a thematic colour. This is not, in actual fact, so novel in itself, but the way it is carried out is really original. The inventor of high-saturation monochromatic theme-windows is Rudolph Steiner, and we can see them if we care to at Dornoch, near Basel, Switzerland, in the giant Goetheanum. They anticipate Chagall by almost fifty years. But they are not works of art, only an addled idea carried out very badly. Chagall conceived the idea of suffusing each separate window with a characteristic theme colour. The whole window was to be dominated by a ground of green or blue or yellow or red, and into this reservoir of primary colour there were projected small areas of highly contrasting colour which floated about (a recurrent phenomenon in Chagall's painting) in the primary soup. Over this colour-shift, which was originally chosen by means of employing collage – different coloured small bits of paper being moved about over the monochrome ground – there was a painted image which sometimes ran parallel to the colour-change, and sometimes cut across it. There seemed always to be some kind of contrapuntal understanding between the two elements of painting and colour but in some areas, where there was an intricate change of colour, a lot of aciding was required. This was not straightforward aciding such as can be done by dumping the stopped-out glass in an acid bath and then removing it, as in etching for example. No, the surface of practically every piece had to be 'mopped', or continually sponged by hand using pure acid on the end of a little mop. (Hence the descriptive name for the process.) It needs little imagination to envisage just how time-consuming and tedious – and vunerable to silly mistakes – this process is, to say nothing about possible health-hazards from accidental inhalation of the deadly acid-gas. It is no surprise that the average Chagall window cost ten times the amount that was charged for windows by other designers. But the end effect justified every sweated hour and every bill submitted.

The effect of colour-saturation such as we see at Jerusalem is interesting enough. The eye is supported by the continuum of the ground colour as in a continuum accompaniment in music, and, relying on that to give it confidence and surety, can then hop about *ad lib* from one little other-coloured island to the next. It is all very satisfactory and pleasant, especially if the eye takes in the incidents

All Saints, Tudely, Kent.
Detail of Crucifixion by
Marc Chagall, mid 20C
(Photo Painton Cowen)

connected to the painted image *en route*. This is the optical organization of a great painter.

Where the quality of the image as a whole is weakened, in my
opinion, is the imposition of the leadwork image. This is not the
work of Chagall himself, rather that of the interpreter, Charles
Marq. There is something repugnant in the almost arbitrary leading
thrown across the delicate designs in a random series of arcs and
lines. This coarsens the painter's image sometimes beyond recognition. The task of matching leadlines to painterly image is one of
the hardest optical tasks for a stained-glass interpreter – especially

180

Varengeville-sur-Mer.
Windows by Georges
Braque, 1950s

BELOW
St Maximim, Metz.
Window designed by Jean
Cocteau, late 20C (Photo
Painton Cowen)

All Saints,
Wellingborough.
Window by Evie Hone,
1955

as there is no one to help him in this matter. The painter-designer cannot do it, being quite unprepared for the task; it is a disaster to leave it to craftsmen. The only solution is to find an interpreter who has as fine a sensibility as the original painter-designer and this is an enormously rare occurrence. The windows that Marc Chagall designed have been seriously modified, and that not to the good, by the choice of leadline character that has been imposed on his window designs.

The simplest things are often the best and the work of Chagall is no exception. His little altar window in the country chapel at Tudely, Kent, in England, is a small masterpiece of sensitivity and pellucid transparency. I do not think the rest of the church's glazing is really up to the quality of the main window. The Chagall window at Chichester Cathedral is not really one of his best; it seems to have been the victim of too much delegation at the end of his career. The reds are glaring and insensitive.

So much for only a tiny fraction of the corpus of late-twentieth-century French glass. It is interesting that the best designs, so far as artists were concerned, were by men who had either directly, or obliquely, been through the harrowing time of the 1939–45 war. The later stars of the Ecole de Paris such as Pierre Soulages and Georges Matthieu did not care to pick up the challenge of stained glass; perhaps they were never encouraged to. Subsequently, during the early 60s, the hegemony of art was wrested from the hands of France and Paris by the crudely vital energy of the school of New York. Its combination of the Abstract Sublime, Pop in all its variations and the Minimalists, spread worldwide by Federal agencies, finally dissolved France's self-confidence. We have yet to see this renewed.

The situation the other side of the channel, in England, was very different from that in France during the thirty years after the 1939–45 war. There was not nearly so much damage, either physical or psychological, as there had been in France. Much had been destroyed, it is true, but when a dispassionate survey is held over the *total* amount of damage done in England it was very considerably less than in France – and bears no comparison whatsoever to that of Germany.

OPPOSITE
Derby Cathedral. All Saints window by Ceri Richards, interpreted by Patrick Reyntiens, 1960s

RIGHT
Decorative panel by Heinrich Campendonk

BELOW
Decorative panel by Jan Thorn-Prikker

Detail of window by Anton Wendling

OPPOSITE Pasing, Munich. Window by Georg Meistermann

186

Birkesdorf Church.
Window by Ludwig
Schaffrath (Photo Ed
Carpenter)

OPPOSITE
Church window at
Kitzingen by Johannes
Schreiter, detail (Photo
Andrew Moor)

Coventry Cathedral had been totally burnt out save for the tower. Plans matured early to rebuild it. The idea was to build a totally new structure while retaining as much of the old fifteenth-century Gothic remains as was deemed feasible. After a few false starts the architect Basil Spence was chosen to design anew, from scratch. He visited two churches already mentioned in this book, Notre Dame du Raincy, outside Paris, and the small church of experimental art at Assy, and from these his basic ideas were formed. The quality of the masonry in the sheer walls of aslar he derived from the quality of stone walls in Scotland, such as Linlithgow Palace, but he also looked at the giant walls from Parma, Cremona and Mantua, in Italy.

Whatever the origins of the design in Coventry Cathedral it is the glass that interests us. The walls each side of the nave going up to the High Altar are stepped in concertina-formation. The viewer approaching the altar sees a large empty expanse of smooth pink ashlar, except for Gospel texts incised into the wall at the base. When the visitor looks back, however, the cathedral tells another story, for only then is one aware of the serried ranges of giant windows, each some seventy-five feet tall, that stalk up the nave, occupying the *other* faces of the concertina-formation. Two by two they come, first a green pair, designed by Keith New, symbolizing childhood, then a red pair for the experiences of hot youth, then a multicoloured pair, presumably for the confusion experienced in middle age. These are followed by a magnificent pair of purple windows designed by Geoffrey Clarke, the best in the church in my view, symbolizing old age and death. Finally there is a pair of golden-coloured ones, representative of the after-life. These were designed by Lawrence Lee. The only drawback to these magnificent windows is that, though they are designated 'symbolic' the actual symbolism is so recondite and obscure that a handbook is needed to explain it all. Symbolism that needs painstaking explanation seems to lose its essential function, for the proper nature of symbolism is to connect with the subconscious, making explanation unnecessary.

The Baptistry window on the right as the church is entered is entirely different. It was commissioned some years after the nave

St Nikolaus, Walbeck. Detail of window by Joachim Klos (Photo Andrew Moor)

191

windows. Since I took three years making it to the designs of John Piper, the British painter, I have a rather too heavy vested interest in it, so I shall not say a lot about it. The extreme difficulty of designing for such a self-defeating window-pattern is evident. Nothing put into the window overcame with any ease the complete camouflaging effect of the masonry cut-offs. The blocks between the glass were simply too big. An explosion of light in the middle was indeed the only answer possible. This window, to the wonderment of the architects, was started at the top and worked downwards, towards the bottom. Architects usually instruct builders to proceed in the opposite direction. However this mode of working enabled both designer and maker to experiment in the values and the style most appropriate to the situation and make adjustments as necessary as the glass approached nearer the human eye. On the whole it worked, but to keep an image of such intricate colour-structure in the mind's eye for over three years is a considerable responsibility.

The revival of interest in stained glass in England is not to be dated from Coventry Cathedral, however important it is for the history of English glass. The real protagonist of the new interest was the Irish designer Evie Hone who studied painting under André Lhote and Albert Gleizes in the derivative cubist tradition of the 1920s in Paris. She was thus able to escape at one leap from the inherent ecclesiastical kitsch which was never far from the surface in Catholic Ireland, and avoid entanglement with the inherited, and rather stodgy values of Protestant England. To an acute eye trained in the ateliers of Paris in the purity of colour that the Ecole de Paris demanded, with its discipline of composition, she allied a Celtic imagination and seriousness of subject-matter. Viewers are in no doubt that the sacred subjects which Evie Hone tackled meant everything to her. This explains the almost uncomfortable feeling one has when confronted with a large window such as was commissioned from her at Eton College Chapel. This great window in a stately, even though incomplete, perpendicular Gothic chapel, was the greatest surprise to the English public.

Evie Hone had quite a few commissions in Britain before she died, the most notable being the east window of St Michael's Highgate,

Eton College Chapel. The Crucifixion and the Last Supper, great east window, by Evie Hone, 1952

London, and two windows of great intensity, one of them a rose, in the Jesuit church at Farm Street, London.

The placing of painters as designers in the world of British stained glass never caught on in the same way as it had under the Church and the Beaux Arts in France. This was largely due to the timidity and the ignorance, I'm afraid, of the clergy, both Anglican and Catholic, as to the possibilities inherent in the world of the contemporary painter in the post-war art scene. It was a case of the two worlds never caring to meet. The sole exception to this melancholy

193

story of omission is John Piper. His first commission was difficult enough to push through, but it had the advantage, like Eton, of being in the hands of a large and famous public school, Oundle, in Northamptonshire, and this kept it out of the somewhat reactionary circles who were apt to control art patronage in the Church of England proper. The three windows, each of three lights, were designed by Piper in a style quite new – yet with distinct and subtly oblique references to thirteenth-century glass, especially that of the clerestory at Bourges Cathedral. The individual faces of the nine figures owe something, if not in form then in inspiration, to those of Picasso's *Les Damoiselles d'Avignon*. The heads are bafflingly abstract, a treatment that does not extend to the hands. Stained glass of this intensity had hitherto not been seen in England except for the work of Evie Hone at Eton. It was therefore logical, on the death of the latter, who left designs for the two flanking windows to the great east window at Eton unrealized, that John Piper should be invited to submit designs for the chapel windows that were not already filled with modern plain glazing. There were eight in all, the Parables up one side (right) and the Miracles up the other (left). The work took four years, each window being some twenty-five feet high and fifteen in width. John Piper proceeded to receive many other commissions in the course of a busy life and he has left his mark on the history of stained glass in England. His was an achievement parallel to that of Marc Chagall in France, but it should never be forgotten that Piper started the process of designing for glass very much ahead of Chagall.

The greatest achievement in John Piper's career as a stained-glass designer is the largest window at Robinson College, Cambridge, in the chapel/concert hall. This was enormously difficult to make and took me two years. Every device that was legitimately called for in the way of technical expertise was put into this commission, and the difficulty of avoiding solecisms in colouring and rhythm were formidable, since, as in the Baptistry window at Coventry Cathedral, one could only see a very small area at any one time during the working process. The smallest window by John Piper is in the little winter chapel attached to the main college chapel. This, of the

Oundle School Chapel.
The Way, the Truth and
the Life, by John Piper
interpreted by Patrick
Reyntiens, 1950s (Photo
Painton Cowen)

St Andrew, Plymouth. St`
Catherine window by
John Piper interpreted by
Patrick Reyntiens, 1960s
(Photo Painton Cowen)

*Adoration of the Magi,* was the most difficult work to do from a technical point of view. No painter keeps to the possibilities of stained glass better than John Piper, yet at the same time no painter stretches his executive interpreter more cruelly.

The most considerable artist to design stained glass, apart from John Piper, in the last thirty years in Britain is the Welsh painter Ceri Richards. Though he did not receive many commissions in the course of his life, the ones he did receive were serious and important. The two windows in Derby Cathedral, England, are set into classical embrasures. The filling of classical, round-headed arches seems always better for the modern designer since the pressure to conform, even obliquely, to the Gothic idiom is always there when filling a Gothic embrasure. This is avoided in filling simple round arches. Unlike Piper, Richards was a painter who had absolutely no feeling for the Gothic whatsoever, and the provision of two large classical windows as at Derby suited him admirably.

The dominant school of stained glass (if it can indeed be called a school) in the modern world is undoubtedly the German. The Reich was totally annihilated at the conclusion of the war, and the homeland of Germany was divided between east and west. So for the first time since the eighteenth century the whole of Germany was not under the influence of Prussia and Berlin. This political renewal and the added fact that the physical shell of town-based civilization was eighty per cent destroyed, initiated the extensive task of totally rebuilding German civilization. The churches as political entities were the only fast and dependable institutions that had survived the destruction of Nazism and it was natural that they constituted the basis from which much flowed. The strength of the position that the churches held in public opinion was the reason so many notable new buildings were erected between 1945 and 1975. Not only churches but secular buildings craved for colour and design other than the rectilinear machine-based aesthetic. As a result an enormous amount of stained glass was commissioned. The south of Germany led the country in this interest in stained glass just as it had two hundred years previously in the pioneering of the new Rococo style.

At first there were masters such as Heinrich Campendonk and Anton Wendling, whose experiences predated the war and who were influenced by the last phase of the Gothic revival in Germany. Their style is highly graphic and compartmentalized and has that definite, almost ruthless quality that one associates with German graphic

Justice Center, Portland, Oregon. Window by Ed Carpenter (Photo Ed Carpenter)

design. Georg Meistermann is a giant in the world of stained-glass design. He broke loose from the vestiges of the Gothic idiom and produced very large windows of breathtaking energy and novelty. His role in the history of German stained glass was almost to pioneer the possibility of a renewal and reinvention of idiom. As such he dominated the German scene for many years. There are so many good names in Germany that it is difficult to pick and choose. Two major artists who followed Meistermann, though not in his footsteps, Ludwig Schaffrath and Johannes Schreiter, will always be known as masters of the post-war scene of stained glass in Germany. Their styles are by no means similar. Schaffrath's art continues to develop to this day. It is a dynamic linear art, which relies far more on the rhythms of the leadwork and the quality of the interval between them for infusing vitality into the window-space than on the colour or the content of the composition. His use of colour is markedly restrained since he notes that the immoral use of colour in advertising techniques and in television distorts the public's self-knowledge of their emotional reaction. So assaulted are they by profligate use of colour, they do not know what to think. The result is that Schaffrath only very rarely uses colour to its fullest extent – and always with a much restricted palette. His best work is in almost monochrome opalescent glass, the statement being advanced only by the subtlest manipulation of tonality and varying degrees of opacity. He paid frequent visits to Japan and this experience seems to have opened his art up to a whole range of further possibilities.

Johannes Schreiter is a painter and Professor of Painting at the Frankfurt Academy. His art is altogether less graphic than that of Schaffrath. His large-scale windows bear a direct relationship to his paintings. The latter are sometimes done in *papier-collé* and the individual bits of paper are charred and burnt, in order to get the effect and the emotional response that he requires. Again the colour is severely limited in the interests of the greater whole. This painterly idiom translates well into stained glass, and it is not surprising that the more painterly the approach, as in Schreiter's chapel at Leutersdorf, the more spectacular and satisfying the effect.

Ray King. Autonomous panel, 1980 (Photo Ray King)

OPPOSITE BELOW
Artpark, Leviston, NY. *Solar Projections* by Ray King 1980 (Photo Ray King)

LEFT
Ludwig Schaffrath. Detail from the Pieper-Haus (Photo Ed Carpenter)

Other names that occur constantly are Jochen Poensgen, a very sure designer in an idiom that owes much to industrial component design. Poensgen is a master of the 'repeat' in glass. That is to say he makes use of the repetition of basic, simple-seeming units that, by some inexplicable magic, add up to far more than the sum of their parts. Wilhem Bosschulte is in the mainstream of renewal in German stained glass. His use of colour is more emancipated than that of Schreiter or Schaffrath, but it is also less controlled.

The most interesting artist to my mind working in the medium is Joachim Klos. He is of the same generation as the other artists I have mentioned but he has a far more enquiring mind. This enquiry entails the re-grasping of the figurative idiom and its re-examination and re-interpretation. To a certain extent Joachim Klos's line of approach is to re-utilize the images of the past, such as lithographics and nineteenth-century reproductions, incorporating them into his windows as a substitute for the figurative basis that should occur. Klos's use of such images is extremely ingenious and his placing of them in relation to the rest of the (non-figurative) window is masterly. Klos is either a very good painter on glass or employs good painters. What he has not so far attempted is a human figure painted by his own hand on glass. There comes a time when the reproduction of someone else's art (from the past), even though this may be an ironic gesture, is not a sufficiently positive commitment.

For there is a crisis in German stained glass for all its accomplishment and success. That is the crisis of what human beings *are* and what they should say to one another to construct a 'good' world. The non-figurative art from the 1950s to the 1980s seems to indicate a profound amnesia. It is almost as though the aesthetic of opalescence in the majority of windows is the aesthetic of bandaged eyes, that of recovery at the convalescent clinic. There is only a certain length of time that can be expended on the art of waiting, bandaged up. The dressings must one day be removed and the flesh revealed. Joachim Klos comes near to doing this.

There is very little private glass, in panel or portable form, in Germany. All work is of large public commissions. But there are exceptions. One artist who has made a particular study and success of this personalized art is von Stockhausen. His larger pieces, the major commissions, are perhaps not as happy as his smaller panels. All the painting is his own autograph and as a result the vitality of the smaller pieces is outstanding.

The contrast between von Stockhausen and the rest of Germany is of interest to us all. It demonstrates the difficulty of our divided art and design worlds. On the one hand 'art' is the triumph of the individual, the prophetic side of man – the liberation of people's aspirations. It is the guarantee of individuality and personal worth. On the other, 'design' is the expression of the sinews of society, of those activities that hold the whole of the fabric of society together. As such, those activities have an overwhelmingly *impersonal* character, and it is the expression of that impersonality that permeates and informs all design-problems. As architecture lies uneasily between the two categories, inclining more to the impersonal than to the personal, it is easy to see that the antipathy between a personalized art, such as painting *is,* and stained glass, in certain circumstances, *should be,* and the machine-finished milieu of architecture today poses very profound problems.

This basic difficulty, connected to the Modern Movement in architecture, is slowly transmuting into a different situation. We have escaped from the Miesian dictum of 'less is more' into the world of Philip Johnson's 'less is a bore'. The going in this respect is largely centred on America which still has the greatest complement of good architects within its borders. The general turn towards re-examining the past, making what use of it when possible and re-introducing some reference into the forms of architecture, whilst avoiding mere uninformed pastiche, is producing a new situation of hope and creative expansion in the world of stained glass in America. Certain artists have been highly successful in the recent past, and have made their presence felt. Ed Carpenter is outstanding in this respect, having many highly successful commissions to his credit. The architectural scene is endowed indeed when a Carpenter window is part of the general expression of the building. Carpenter inclines to the architectural and the design-centred ethos of stained glass rather than the private or the painterly. His work is a subtle bridge between the

Ed Carpenter. Panel in
private residence, 1976
(Photo Ed Carpenter)

Ray King, *Ghost Shield III*, 1979 (Photo Ray King)

individuality of the artist and the demands of an impersonal touch associated with the needs of American architecture.

Ray King is an artist in glass who is highly individual in his approach. His skill in cutting and in leading-up is such that it is impossible to delegate what he conceives as an artist. The perfection of the craft is subsumed into the expression of the art and no one is capable of putting a fake Ray King on the market, since they simply do not possess a matching skill. King invented the domestic statement in glass in his hanging pieces. These are an original application of the autonomous panel, since they float in the interior. Made in opalescent and translucent glass they may be read from either side with differing effect. King is master of the interior fitting, combining electricity with stained glass and metalwork.

Richard Posner is an individual artist whose work at San Francisco Science Pavilion deserves more notice. The delicacy of his statement depends on minutely adjusted calculations involving aciding. A new realism with slightly surrealist overtones seems to be the order of the day. Posner again tackles the problem of relating stained glass to architecture.

RIGHT
Ray King, *Icon I*, 1978
(Photo Ray King)

OPPOSITE
Robert Kehlmann,
*Composition XXXIX*
(Photo Robert Kehlmann)

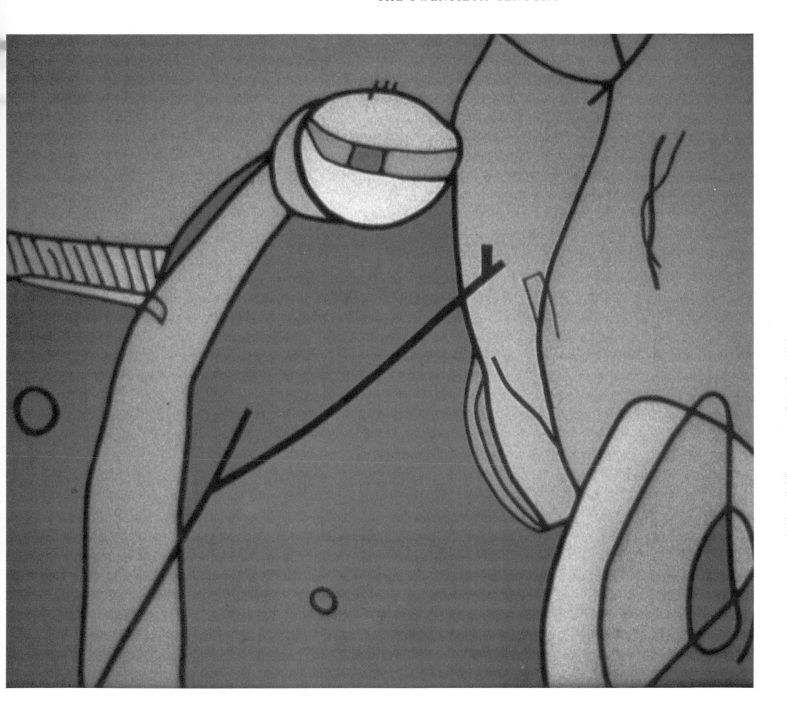

Rannoch School,
Scotland. Detail of
window by Douglas
Hogg, 1983 (Photo
Douglas Hogg)

OPPOSITE
Robert Kehlmann,
*Composition XXXXII*
(Photo Robert Kehlmann)

OVERLEAF ABOVE LEFT
Exhibition panel, lunette,
*Leto and the frogs*, 1984
by Patrick Reyntiens.
Private collection (Photo
Michael Le Marchant,
Bruton Gallery, Bruton,
Somerset)

OVERLEAF BELOW LEFT
*Hommage à Berlioz*,
autonomous panel, detail,
by Patrick Reyntiens,
1985

OVERLEAF RIGHT
*Orpheus charming the
trees*, detail. Panel by
Patrick Reyntiens. Private
collection (Photo Michael
Le Marchant, Bruton
Gallery, Bruton,
Somerset)

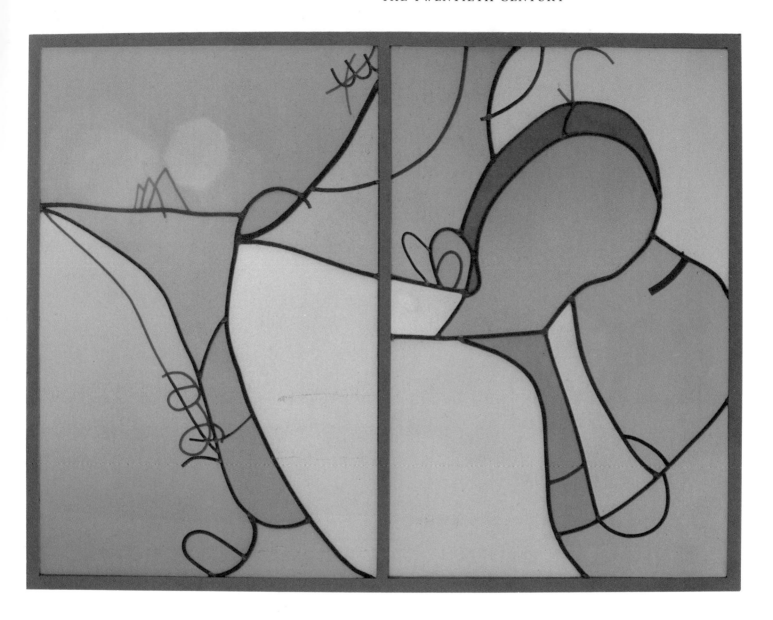

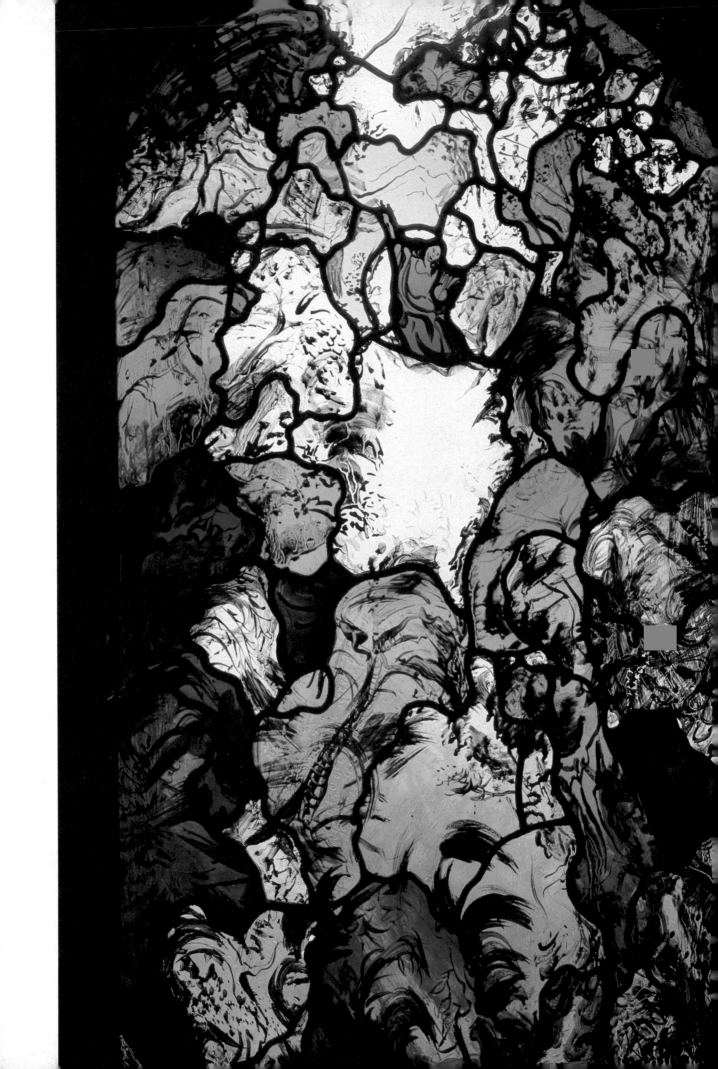

St Edward the Confessor,
Chandler's Ford,
Southampton.
*Resurrection*, window by
David Wasley, 1990 (Photo
Malcolm Crowthers)

*Spectral Screen.*
Exhibition window by
Brian Clarke, 1988 (Photo
Andrew Moor)

**OPPOSITE**
St John's Church,
Wanstead, Essex. *Closed
Paradise*, window by
Patrick Reyntiens, 1970s

**LEFT**
*A Dream of Kristellnacht*
by Rosalind Grimshaw
(Photo Rosalind
Grimshaw)

OPPOSITE
St John's church,
Johannesburg. Baptistry
window by Brian Young
(Photo Brian Young)

LEFT
St David's, Hendy, Dyfed.
St Sebastian window by
Graham Jones (Photo
Andrew Moor)

# Envoi

The England of Coventry Cathedral and Liverpool Metropolitan Cathedral is now relegated to history. A new generation is arising of whom Graham Jones is perhaps the most promising. Within the last fifteen years there have been outstanding talents whose opportunities are largely outside England. Brian Clarke is the most prominent example. His work is known from Arabia to Japan and New York. Clarke's idiom is that of the medieval chivalry clash of primary colours brought up to date. It is public art on a public scale. Alexander Beleschenko is an adept at designing a window or sculpture to fit modern architecture as a perfect complement.

The growth of the stained-glass panel as an autonomous art object is as yet in its infancy but pioneer work being done by Rosalind Grimshaw, Douglas Hogg, David Wasley and others will surely make a mark on the art scene sooner or later. This development, which is of particular interest to me and in which I share, may well be the point at which new ideas in glass, ideas connected to painting and not necessarily entirely in thrall to architecture, will once again succeed in forging something original and vivifying.

# Selected Bibliography

ANGUS, M. *Modern stained glass in British churches* 1984

CLARKE, B. (ed.) *Architectural stained glass* 1979

COE, B. *Stained glass in England and Wales* 1980

DONNELY, M. *Glasgow stained glass: a preliminary study* 1981

FARMER, O. G. *Fairford church and its stained glass windows* 1962

Glasgow Art Gallery and Museum *Stained and painted glass in the Burrell Collection* 1965

HARRISON, K. P. *The windows of King's College Chapel, Cambridge* 1952

HARRISON, M. *Victorian stained glass* 1980

HOLIDAY, H. *Stained glass as an art* 1896

LE COUTEUR, J. D. *English Medieval painted glass* 1926

LEE, L. *The appreciation of stained glass* 1977

NELSON, P. *Ancient painted glass in England, 1170–1500* 1913

PIPER, J. *Stained glass: art or anti-art* 1968

REYNTIENS, P. *The technique of stained glass* 1977

SAN CASCIANI, P. & P. *The stained glass of Oxford* 1982

SKEAT, F. W. *The stained glass windows of St Albans Cathedral* 1977

## TECHNICAL

WINSTON, C. *Art of glass painting* John Murray, London 1865

TWINING, E. W. *The art and craft of stained glass* Pitman & Sons 1928

LE VIEIL, M. *L'art de la peinture sur verre et de la vitrerie* Paris 1774

WHALL, C. H. *Stained glass work* John Hogg, London 1905

Anon. *Hints of glass painting, parts 1 & 2* Parker, Oxford 1847

## HISTORICAL

WOODFORDE, C. *The Norwich School of glass painting* Oxford University Press 1950

WOODFORDE, C *The stained glass of New College, Oxford* Oxford University Press 1951

WOODFORDE, C. *English stained and painted glass* Clarendon Press 1954

WHITE, JAMES & WYNNE, MICHAEL *Irish stained glass* Furrow Trust, Dublin 1963

LEWIS, F. DAY *Windows: a book about stained glass* Batsford 1909

DELAPORTE, L'ABBÉ *Les Vitraux de la Cathédrale de Chartres, Text and Vols 1, 2, 3* E. Houvet, Chartres 1926

EDEN, F. SYDNEY *Ancient stained and painted glass* Cambridge University Press 1933

HARRISON, F. *The painted glass of York* SPCK 1927

HARRISON, F. *Stained glass of York Minster* The Studio Ltd, London

KNOWLES, JOHN F. *The York School of Glass Painting* 1936

MAGNE, M. LUCIEN *Musée retrospectif de la classe '67 Vitraux*

MARCHINI, G. *Italian stained glass windows* Thames & Hudson, London 1957

RACKHAM, BERNARD *Ancient glass of Canterbury Cathedral* Lund Humphries

READ, HERBERT *English stained glass* Putnams, London 1926

RITTER, GEORGE *Les Vitraux de la Cathédral de Rouen* Cognac 1926

SHERRILL, CHARLES HITCHCOCK *Stained glass tours in France* John Lane, London 1909

SHERILL, CHARLES HITCHCOCK *Stained glass tours in England* John Lane/Bodley Head 1909

SHERILL, CHARLES HITCHCOCK *Stained glass tours in Italy* John Lane/Bodley Head 1913

SHERILL, CHARLES HITCHCOCK *Stained glass tours in Spain and Flanders* John Lane/Bodley Head 1924

SHERRILL, CHARLES HITCHCOCK *Stained glass tours in Austria, Germany & the Rhinelands* Bodley Head 1927

SOWERS, R. *The lost art* Zwemmer

SOWERS, R. *Stained glass: an architectural art* Zwemmer

ARNOLD, HUGH *Stained glass of the Middle Ages* Black, London 1913

BEYER, V. *Stained glass windows* Oliver & Boyd, London 1964

GUITARD, S. CLEMENT A. *Vitraux de Bourges* Tardy-Pigelet, Bourges 1900

CONNICK, CHARLES *Adventures in light and colour* Harrap 1937

SEWTER, A. C. *The stained glass of William Morris and his circle, vols I & II* Yale University Press 1975

ANTIQUARIAN

WESTLAKE, N. H. J. *A history of design in painted glass, vols I, II, III & IV* James Parker 1894

DRAKE, MAURICE *A history of English glass painting* T. Werner Laurie Ltd., London 1912

HUCHER, EUGENE *Folio. Vitraux peints Cathédrale du Mans* Didron, Paris 1865

LASTEYRIE, FERDINAND DE *Histoire de la peinture sur verre, vols 1 & 2* Didot frères, Paris 1853

VERRIER, JEAN *Vitraux de France, Twelfth and Thirteenth Centuries.* Histoire des arts Plastiques, Paris

BOISSONET, C. H. *Les Verriers de la Cathédrale de Tours* Paris 1932

CHAGALL, MARC, text, LEYMARIE, J. *The Jerusalem Windows* André Sauret, Monaco 1962

STETTLER, MICHAEL *Swiss stained glass of the Fourteenth Century* Batsford 1949

AUBERT, MARCEL *Stained glass of the Twelfth and Thirteenth Century French cathedrals* Batsford 1951

BAKER, J. & LAMMER, A. *English stained glass* Thames & Hudson 1960

AHNNE, PAUL *Vitraux de la Cathédrale de Strasbourg* Strasbourg 1960

# Index

Figures in italics refer to illustrations